Make Life Successful

Anil B. Sarkar, PhD

© Blossoms Books 2018. All rights reserved.

Dedication

This book is dedicated to Lord Krishna, Sri Krishna Chaitanya Mahaprabhu, Srila Prabhupada and Paramahansa Yogananda.

The following poem was written to encourage my daughter, and all of my descendants, in moments of uncertainty and anxiety, and to let them know there is no need to worry; life will be good in Krishna consciousness.

Fly High Little Bird

Be not afraid little bird, ye shall fly high.
Ye shall soar high.

The storm will pass.
The darkness will end.
The morning will come.
The sun will rise.

Thy drenched wings will dry.
Ye will soar.
And ye will fly.

Ye shall fly over the hills and the vales.
Ye shall fly over the rivers,
And the wind will take ye to the glowing sky.

Table of Contents

Dedication	i
Fly High Little Bird	iii
Introduction	1
Philosophy	4
Philosophy for this Age	13
Process	32
Mantra Meditation	58
Royal Knowledge	80
Bhakti Yoga	92
The Light of the Gita	105
Conclusion	135
108 Questions and Answers	137
Glossary	156
My Story	162

Introduction

All living entities, humans, animals, plants, aquatics and insects are always searching for happiness. We all wish to be healthy, live a prosperous life and have no anxiety and stress. Like little bees constantly flying about in search of honey, we are also restlessly seeking our desires. For bees, finding honey will make them happy. For ants, finding sugar will make them happy. For trees, sunshine and water will make them happy. For human beings, however, the platform of happiness is different. Being healthy, wealthy and knowledgeable are certainly conducive to a good life, but one also needs to be on a higher level of consciousness. That level of consciousness is transcendental, or Krishna consciousness.

In Krishna consciousness, one's mind is immersed in thoughts of Krishna. One thinks of Krishna's beauty, His words as in *The Bhagavad Gita* (BG) or His attributes and pastimes as narrated in *The Srimad Bhagavatam* (SB) and *The Chaitanya Charitamrita* (CC). In Krishna consciousness, one's mind is clear, calm and peaceful as an autumn sky. One becomes a devotee, and understands that Krishna in His Vāsudeva form is everything. Thus being in tune with Krishna, who is the God of gods, one's consciousness becomes full of unlimited potential and knowledge. One will transcend the mundane world of the three modes of material nature (*guna*s), which are goodness, passion, and ignorance. One becomes joyful and happy.

Krishna consciousness is always present in everyone's heart. It can be awakened in a pure heart by the nine processes of bhakti, namely: hearing about Krishna, chanting His Holy Names, remembering Krishna, serving Him, worshipping Him, offering prayers, working as a servitor of Krishna, developing a friendship with Him and surrendering to Krishna's lotus feet. By chanting the Maha Mantra (*Hare Krishna, Hare Krishna, Krishna Krishna, Hare Hare; Hare Rama, Hare Rama, Rama Rama, Hare Hare*), reading *The Bhagavad Gita* and eating *prasadam*, one can easily awaken one's dormant love of God.

One can practice Krishna consciousness at any stage of life. If one sincerely chants the Holy Names, one's life will be perfect; one will be liberated from the three modes of material nature. One does not have to leave society or give up one's duty to become Krishna conscious. All one needs to do is live a pure life and chant the Lord's name with devotion. If one can start devotional service from childhood, it is better because children's minds are pure and they are not entangled in material life. Prince Dhruva and Prince Prahlad became devotees at an early age and saw and spoke to Krishna face to face. Prince Dhruva became a righteous King and after leaving his body went to his own planet, Dhruva Loka (the Pole Star). Prince Prahlad became the ruler of the three worlds and ruled for 36,000 years.

The Bhagavad Gita points out that we are not our bodies but spiritual particles, and the whole spirit is Lord Krishna. When we understand this truth, we no longer work for our body's sense gratification. We now work for our spiritual body or soul, which is eternal, full of knowledge and bliss. We become Krishna conscious; we become persons of steady wisdom. In the bodily platform we are *sammohita jiva* or illusioned living entities. To live fully, one needs to be Krishna conscious. Krishna consciousness means to be linked with Krishna in thought, words and deeds in a mood of devotion.

In Krishna consciousness, our human qualities such as compassion and wisdom become more acute and manifested. One becomes calm, peaceful, detached and happy. One feels a connection with everyone and everything. One becomes tolerant and empathetic. One views people and things with great clarity and waves of joy throb in one's heart. When one is in Krishna consciousness, one can have an actual experience of one's inner nature or the truth of life. One will have insight (*prajna*) about everything and one will be enlightened. One will be healthy, wealthy and wise effortlessly. By connecting one's consciousness with the Supreme consciousness, one's life will be perfect and successful.

Sri Chaitanya Mahaprabhu, who appeared as an avatar of Krishna in Bengal in 1486, said that if one is born in the holy land of India, one should make one's life successful by Krishna consciousness, and help others (*"janma sarthak kori"* —CC Adi 9.41). At one point the whole earth was known as India, or Bharat. Therefore, all the inhabitants of the earth should make their lives successful by practicing Krishna consciousness. The goal of human life is to help others (humans, animals, plants, insects and aquatics) to become God conscious or Krishna conscious, which is the ultimate welfare work.

Philosophy

Krishna consciousness is our pure consciousness. It is also our original consciousness. If someone wants to be happy and live a great life, he must return to his pure consciousness. At present, our consciousness is impure. It is full of ignorance, anxiety, worries and many negative emotions. One's unalloyed consciousness is the true foundation of one's life. Krishna consciousness may be defined as full awareness of Krishna or God. The process of awakening our devotion and love for Krishna is also Krishna consciousness.

The orderliness of the universe, the laws of action and reaction, the conservation of energy, and the infiniteness of the universe certainly point to a gigantic power at work. This power is preservative in nature. Nothing gets annihilated; only the form can change. We can understand it is all good, as it sustains and conserves. It is harmonious, balanced and interconnected with all things and beings.

As our human body is powered by the soul, the universe is powered by a Supersoul. As human beings are persons, so is the Supersoul. His name is Krishna. Krishna means "all attractive." His all attractiveness keeps the universe together and in order. All things and beings (including ourselves) emanate from Krishna. Because we have personality, therefore, God must also have a personality, as the whole cannot have less than a part of itself. The universe, with all its living and material entities, follows Sanatana Dharma, or the Eternal Law, set forth by Lord Krishna. It is therefore our duty to harmonize our activities with this universal principle. We can make our lives perfect by simply following the instructions given by Lord Krishna in *The Bhagavad Gita*. Krishna has instructed us to surrender ourselves to Him, meaning we should tune in our activities with Him.

The process of Krishna consciousness is straightforward and very pleasurable to execute. One has to chant 16 rounds of the Maha Mantra every day; eat *prasadam* (vegetarian food offered to Lord Krishna); read *The Bhagavad Gita*, *The Chaitanya Charitamrita*, and *The Srimad Bhagavatam*; perform daily worship; visit temples and places of pilgrimage; and be compassionate to all living entities. If one diligently follows these six principles, one's dormant Krishna consciousness will be awakened and one's life will be sublime and perfect. By mantra meditation we can focus our attention on Krishna and be immersed in devotion and offer our love to Him: *Hare Krishna, Hare Krishna, Krishna Krishna, Hare Hare, Hare Rama, Hare Rama, Rama Rama, Hare Hare.*

The benefits of Krishna consciousness are immediate; by chanting the Holy Names we bring Krishna in our heart and the forest fire of *samsara* (or material life) is at once extinguished. One starts to become happy right away and one's consciousness, thoughts, mindset and beliefs change to become universal. One gradually becomes healthy, wealthy, wise and happy. One becomes creative, a critical thinker, has high self-esteem, looks youthful and is compassionate; one lives one's life with a thrill. There are no stringent rules or regulations for the chanting of the Maha Mantra. One may continue to do the work one is doing but add the regular chanting of the Maha Mantra to one's daily routine. One can chant in any place at any time. Lord Chaitanya Mahaprabhu said that one simply needs to chant the Hare Krishna Maha Mantra. This mantra is like a wish-fulfilling jewel. By being devoted to Lord Krishna and chanting Hare Krishna, one attains the highest perfection of life. Chaitanya Mahaprabhu said one should chant *Krishna nam* (Krishna's name) and be kind to others (*jive daya*). Krishna conscious life is a life of high thinking and plain living. Our thoughts are always transcendental and our activities are always favourable to Krishna consciousness. We feel friendly to all living entities, especially plants and animals. We have goodwill towards all human beings.

Chanting is a very powerful process. Our consciousness forgets the past and future, and abides in the present moment or Eternal Now. One's worries and regrets are burnt up. Regular chanting of 16 rounds (one round is 108 chants of the Maha Mantra), which is a total of 1,728 times, in a devotional mood brings about a revolution in consciousness (*paravritti* or spiritual awakening) and elevates one to a different plane. Our mind and intelligence elevate to their natural state; one is in a higher cognitive and emotive state. In this state any decision will be correct. It opens the door of all material and spiritual success. Chanting connects us to the Absolute Truth or the Supreme Person, Krishna. It will solve all the problems of material and spiritual life. One may encounter difficulties, but one will nicely overcome them all by Krishna's mercy. Krishna changes the destiny of a surrendered soul. These souls will always be victorious.

Devotees of Lord Krishna do not have problems; they have challenges, which they will overcome.

Our guru, Srila A.C. Bhaktivedanta Swami Prabhupada said that if one keeps one's mind on Krishna, one's body and words will also be on Krishna. All activities will be charged with the power of Krishna. For example, if one puts an iron rod in fire, the rod gradually becomes hotter and hotter, until it becomes red hot and it acquires the quality of fire itself. This is the state of Krishna consciousness. If we succeed in keeping our mind on Krishna, our thoughts, words and deeds will be Krishnized; we acquire the same state as that of Krishna (*bhava*). Our very existence will be sublime and blissful.

Our human life is meant for God realization. That is our only business, and not sensual enjoyment and accumulation of wealth and power, because material enjoyment is temporary and tiresome. One must know the true nature of oneself and the world. One must know the cause of life, death, old age, and disease. Why are we here? Where do we go after death? What is the meaning of life? What is the significance of our existence? One must know the answers to questions like these. Knowledge begins with knowing oneself. As Socrates said, "know thyself." This is the beginning of actual education. Knowledge of Krishna is the ultimate knowledge, and all other knowledge is subordinate to Krishna consciousness, because it only points to Krishna. When one knows Krishna, one knows everything. When one knows the truth of oneself, that one is a spirit soul and related to the Supersoul or God, then one's true education begins.

In the beginning we were souls that were part and parcel of Krishna, in devotion to Krishna in Goloka Vrindavana, our transcendental home with Krishna.

Krishna is like the full moon and the individual souls are like the innumerable stars surrounding the moon. As a part of God, some souls had a desire to enjoy the material world. God acquiesced and in His compassion He agreed to accompany us in the same way a father takes his children where they desire to go. Krishna accompanies us as the Supersoul that dwells in each body with the soul.

Unfortunately, living entities under the three modes of material nature have forgotten their true identity and have become implicated in the material world. According to each soul's desires they continue to reincarnate life after life in various species of living entities. Our duty is to reawaken our original consciousness of being part and parcel of Krishna and our devotion to Him, and return home (Goloka Vrindavana), where we are eternal servitors of Krishna. If we make a wrong turn, Krishna will guide us as a GPS recalculates a new route and directs lost souls to the correct destination.

Lord Chaitanya Mahaprabhu (CC Madhya 20.108) said that *"jīvera 'svarūpa' haya—kṛṣṇera 'nitya-dāsa,' kṛṣṇera 'taṭasthā-śakti' 'bhedābheda-prakāśa.'"* (A living entity's constitutional position is to serve Krishna. Living entities are marginal potencies of Krishna which are simultaneously one and different from Krishna.)

In Krishna consciousness, one's spiritual knowledge and one's material knowledge (arts, science, engineering, medicine, math, etc.) will be perfect. Both material and spiritual knowledge are part of Krishna. In

The Bhagavad Gita, Krishna said that *jnanis* (knowledge seekers) are very dear to Him. One should not neglect material knowledge, as it is necessary for living in the world, as well as to develop Krishna consciousness. One needs to work to earn a living, gain knowledge and live a healthy life. One must know addition and subtraction (material knowledge) before proceeding to higher mathematics (spiritual knowledge). Without knowledge, life does not blossom and a person remains in *raja guna* and *tama guna* (states of passion and ignorance, respectively). In devotional service, one's consciousness will be on a higher plane, and all one's endeavours, material or spiritual, will be successful. Human beings are a special creation; we shouldn't endeavour for sensory happiness, but rather for transcendental happiness.

When we are not in Krishna consciousness, we are in our ego consciousness, which is made of body, mind and intelligence. Ego is developed and controlled by material nature. Material nature consists of three modes: the mode of goodness (*sattva*, which leads to happiness), the mode of passion (*raja*, which leads to misery) and the mode of ignorance (*tama*, which leads to darkness and inertia). The people we are today are the products of different situations and conditions under the three modes of material nature. The conditions of life are always changing. The ego is unable to keep up with the changing conditions and therefore always makes mistakes. However, if we manage to be in our original consciousness, which is full of knowledge and wisdom, our actions will be correct and we will go through life without difficulty. Our body or ego will still be present, but spiritualized, and the Supersoul will guide our lives. By the process of chanting, our senses, mind, and intellect are purified and become friends of our true nature or soul. We will be truly happy; our gain will be unmatched (*"yam labdhva caparam labham"*—BG 6.20–23). There is no greater gain than Krishna consciousness. We will be successful now and beyond.

Krishna consciousness is absolutely essential for attaining perfection. If one wishes to be happy and successful, one must know the truth of life, the world and the universe at large. If one is not aware of one's true self (the *atman*, or soul) and the Supreme Self (Paramatma, or Krishna), or one's position and one's relationship within the cosmos, all one's endeavours will fail, because one's mind will be in the mode of ignorance.

When Krishna consciousness arises in one's heart, the darkness accumulated over millions of lives will vanish in a flash (*Maya andhakar*). As it says in *The Chaitanya Charitamrita* (CC Madhya 22.31), "*kṛṣṇa—sūrya-sama; māyā haya andhakāra. Yāhāṅ kṛṣṇa, tāhāṅ nāhi māyāra adhikāra.*" Krishna will give divine intelligence and be the guide, as He says, "*dadami buddhi-yogam tam*" (BG 10.10). One will know everything, material and spiritual, and attain victory, opulence, extraordinary power, and morality (BG 18.78). In ordinary terms, one will be healthy, wealthy, wise and blissful. It is only natural for us to worship Krishna because we are part of Him. God is great, infinite; we are small, infinitesimal. We are like a small part of a big machine, like nuts and bolts. If we fall out of the machine, we become useless. But in the machine we are in the right place, a part of the working machine, and thus very valuable and meaningful.

By properly understanding oneself as pure existence or Brahman (soul), one can be freed from all material contamination and karma, according to the Svetasvatara Upanishad (3.8). By knowing one's spiritual position or seeing oneself as one actually is, one can attain perfection. One can know the truth that one is a particle of Parabrahman or Krishna and one's duty is to serve Him eternally. One can be free from all contaminations and limitations. Deep understanding of *aham Brahmasmi* (I am spirit or soul) cuts the knot of material attraction.

Our mind is higher than the senses or body, and the intelligence is higher than the mind. One's spirit is higher than the intelligence and is transcendental to the material world. Ordinary people are on the bodily or sensory platform; business people are on the mental platform and engaged in profit making. Scientists and philosophers are on the intellectual platform and they wish to know facts or truth. Devotees of Krishna are on a transcendental plane; their body, mind and intelligence are all engaged in the service of the Lord. Our body, senses, mind and intelligence are material and are subjected to the three modes of material nature, but our soul is spiritual. In Krishna consciousness, not only are our thoughts on the transcendental plane, but even the food offered to Krishna (*prasadam*) that we eat, is transcendental. The devotees have a higher taste in everything.

A devotee should include daily deity worship in their life in order to develop a personal relationship with Krishna. One cannot love someone that one doesn't know. To develop a relationship one needs to exchange food, gifts and conversation. One should offer water, milk, food, incense, flowers and light to Krishna and ring a bell in front of the deity. One can open one's heart to the deity, and share one's gratitude and concerns. At the beginning of a devotee's *sadhana* (spiritual practice), Krishna is not visible to the devotee. Out of mercy, Krishna takes the deity form to allow the devotee to personally connect with Him. Worshipping the deity is the same as worshipping Krishna in person. One can experience Krishna's help and one's gratitude is deepened. Deity worship is a very delightful experience as one receives instant benediction. Srila Prabhupada said God is a person like you and me. By offering these things we develop love or bhakti for Krishna.

When we worship Krishna, He takes charge of our lives, because we are dear to Him, even if we have a huge load of karma. A devotee is in Krishna and Krishna is in the devotee's heart (SB: 9.4.68). He will mitigate or totally negate our karma (*"karmani nirdahati"*— Brahma Samhita 5.54). Krishna will look after our material and spiritual welfare (*"na me bhaktah pranasyati"*—BG 9.31). Our fear, anxieties, lust and greed will gradually disappear from our consciousness, which will become clear like the sunny blue sky and we will be happy and blissful. Everything becomes beautiful and perfect in Krishna's presence. In Krishna consciousness, life becomes a melody.

Philosophy for this Age

In *The Srimad Bhagavatam*, the great sage Sukadev Goswami said to Maharaja Pariksit that Kali Yuga is very inauspicious and full of misery; however, its great quality is that by chanting the Holy Name of Krishna people can attain perfection and success. The material world revolves through four *yugas* or ages: Satya, Treta, Dvapara and the current Kali Yuga. In Satya Yuga, many people were in the mode of goodness and lived long lives. There was an abundance of the necessities of life. The process of self-realization was meditation on Vishnu. In Treta Yuga, people attained self-realization through *yajna*, or fire sacrifice. In Dvapara Yuga, the process of self-realization was through worshipping the Lord. In Kali Yuga, people are mainly in *raja* and *tama gunas*. They have a shorter lifespan and the necessities of life are scarce. It was recommended by Lord Sri Krishna Chaitanya Mahaprabhu to perform *sankirtana* (publicly singing and chanting the names of Krishna) to attain self-realization. He made the process for God realization simple for us. By simply taking the Holy Name of Krishna one can attain all perfection: *"ihā haite sarva-siddhi haibe tomāra"* — *Shikshashtakam*, the only known song personally written by Sri Chaitanya Mahaprabhu.

Ego consciousness or material consciousness is a state of illness from which we can be cured by becoming Krishna conscious. The Holy Name of the Lord acts like a medicine to cure our material consciousness. For example, when one has a fever one talks and thinks incoherently, but when the fever has lifted, then one returns to one's normal consciousness.

Chanting the Holy Name of the Lord is the best method of self-realization for this age. Sri Chaitanya Mahaprabhu said, "In this age of quarrel and hypocrisy, the only means of deliverance is the chanting of the Holy Name of the Lord. There is no other way. There is no other way. There is no other way." (*"Harer nama harer nama harer namaiva kevalam kalau nasty eva nasty eva nasty eva gatir anyatha"* —CC Adi 17.21.)

Chanting forces our mind to focus on Krishna. We should chant in front of a picture of Krishna or His deities. Chanting is pleasurable and is easier to perform than meditation. The method of meditation is difficult because our minds are restless and flickering. However, one may meditate on Krishna after chanting. Chanting immediately raises our consciousness to the transcendental level. The Holy Name also purifies our body, mind and intelligence. The Holy Name puts an orb of golden light around our pure self; thus our existence and Krishna consciousness is always protected.

If a person is in Krishna consciousness, Lord Krishna takes charge of his or her life (*"yoga kshemam bahamyaham"* —BG 9.22). All one's activities are guided by the Supersoul or Paramatma. No error can occur because one is absorbed in the thought of Krishna during these activities. All activities performed in Krishna consciousness are *yajna* or sacrifices; the activities may be gardening, reading, cleaning, cooking, etc.; all one's works are sacrifices (*"brahmarparam brahma havir"* —BG 4.24). Anything one does in pure consciousness is purifying and transcendental. It is beyond the three *gunas*.

Lord Krishna and His Name are non-different (*"avinnatvan nama naminoh"*—Padma Purana). The Holy Name of Krishna is transcendentally blissful and gives eternal liberation. The Maha Mantra is very powerful in removing material contaminations or the effects of the three *gunas* (*"ceto darpana marjanam"*—*Shikshashtakam*). It is even more powerful than Krishna Himself because it works like a medicine from within to cure the material disease (*bhava roga*). When one chants the Holy Names, one gradually develops a taste (*ruci*) for it. By studying *The Bhagavad Gita*, *The Srimad Bhagavatam* and *The Chaitanya Charitamrita*, and associating with other devotees of Krishna, one advances further. One becomes very truthful because God is the Absolute Truth. One also becomes kind and compassionate to all living entities, because all living entities are part and parcel of Krishna. Knowledge of Krishna makes one joyful, *prasannatma* (calm) and clear sighted. One knows the truth of one's own existence and the existence of the universe.

Lord Krishna is Bhagavan (*"kṛṣṇas tu bhagavān svayam"*—SB 1.3.28). He has all six opulences (*bhaga*), namely: wealth, strength, fame, beauty, knowledge and renunciation (*aisvarya*, *viryasya*, *yasha*, *sriya*, *jnana*, *vairagya*). He has invested His potencies in His Holy Name, Krishna. That's why *"Hare Krishna, Hare Krishna, Krishna Krishna, Hare Hare, Hare Rama, Hare Rama, Rama Rama, Hare Hare"* is the greatest mantra. If someone sincerely and submissively chants the Holy Name, one easily attains perfection and becomes Krishna conscious. One should chant in the *Brahma bhuta* state (knowing one is not the body but spirit soul) without any thought of the material world. When one is in the *Brahma bhuta* state, one enjoys happiness from within and one is simply joyful. Krishna consciousness (devotional remembrance) gives us a perfect vantage point, not only for spiritual life but also for material life. Krishna consciousness is our polestar; we will be guided to our destination safely despite the storms of difficulties we may encounter. Krishna will guide our lives through ups and downs, happiness and sadness; the light of Krishna will always be with us.

Taking shelter of the Holy Name solves all the problems of life, material or spiritual, because one is in the correct state of mind. One can see things in the proper perspective and make correct decisions. One becomes pure and wise simply by hearing and chanting Krishna's name (*"puṇya-śravaṇa-kīrtanaḥ"*—SB 1.2.17). At the lotus feet of Krishna (*upasritya*) one is safe, because one is sheltered by Krishna Himself and beyond the three modes of material nature. All obstacles (*sarva durgani*) are easily overcome (BG 18.57–58). When one surrenders to God, Krishna, all one's anxieties evaporate. One comes home and abides in one's transcendental abode. One is back in one's natural condition.

If one takes the Holy Names in a mood of devotion and faith (*shraddha*), eats food offered to Krishna and reads *The Sri Chaitanya Charitamrita* and *The Bhagavad Gita*, one becomes Krishnized. When one becomes fully absorbed in Krishna consciousness, one becomes constitutionally the same as Krishna (*achintya-bheda-abheda*). When one thinks of Krishna constantly, love for Him manifests in the heart (*"bhāvite bhāvite kṛṣṇa sphuraye antare"*—CC Madhya 19.236). By constantly thinking of Krishna the caterpillar of our existence turns into a butterfly of eternal devotion to Krishna. Krishna is the Supreme Person full of kindness and love. He always responds to His devotees. Serving Krishna is different from worldly service. Worldly service makes one tired, but service to Krishna is joyful and refreshing.

Sacrifice or *yajna* for Krishna must be performed, otherwise one will be entangled in sinful material activity and there will be no hope for peace, happiness or liberation. Whatever one does, whatever one eats, all activities should be performed as *yajna* or sacrifice. For our age the recommended *yajna* is *sankirtan yajna*, which is chanting of *Hare Krishna, Hare Krishna, Krishna Krishna, Hare Hare, Hare Rama, Hare Rama, Rama Rama, Hare Hare*, as prescribed by Lord Sri Krishna Chaitanya Mahaprabhu. By this process we can completely purify ourselves from material contamination. Without being in Krishna consciousness, it is not possible to see Krishna, who is God. By Krishna consciousness one obtains divine eyes (*divya chakshu*). Even Arjuna had to be given divine eyes to see the Universal Form of the Lord, though he was a close friend of Sri Krishna (BG 11.8). One cannot see or know God (*"jñātum draṣṭum"* —BG 11.54), nor understand God, without being a pure devotee.

Chanting of the Holy Names is very efficacious for removing the illusion of Maya. We can be immediately purified to the stage of offenseless chanting. However, bhakti (devotional love of Krishna), pure taste and pure feeling come after doing some *sadhana* (spiritual work); one should hear, chant and meditate on Krishna. Chanting, hearing and reading about Krishna are the main pillars of bhakti yoga. Studying the *shastras* (scriptures) deepens our understanding of *dharma, karma, jnana* and *moksha*. One with deep understanding of the Vedas will soon be a pure devotee and will realize one's relationship with the Supreme. Deep knowing of Krishna is the same as seeing Krishna, as Krishna is Absolute. When one knows Krishna, one will feel the presence of God anywhere, anytime, as Krishna is within us as the Supersoul.

Our soul is eternal. From life to life we try to attain perfection, that is, to become a pure devotee. It is only natural for the soul to long for Krishna, like a child longs to be with his mother. The soul being spiritual energy, never dies. It reincarnates time after time until it becomes a pure devotee of Krishna, which is the constitutional position of the soul. We should do our best to develop Krishna consciousness in this current life. Even if we don't fully succeed, we will carry spiritual conceptions and attainments from this life to the next. There will be no spiritual loss or diminution; in fact, we will start our next life from where we ended our previous spiritual life. Thus, one will be in a very favourable position to continue one's *sadhana*.

The transcendental vibration of the Harinam (name of God) from Krishna's flute emanates from Goloka Vrindavana and enters one's heart through one's ears. By chanting the Holy Names and living a *sattvic* life one keeps Krishna at the center of one's life, as one did before one entered this material world. At that time one's existence was full of knowledge and bliss (*sat cit ananda*). At present, one's consciousness is covered with ignorance and it has neither knowledge nor *ananda* (joy). But by the nine processes of devotional service (*sravanam, kirtanam, Vishnu smaranam, padasevanam, archanam, vandanam, dasyam, sakhyam, atmanivedanam*), one can fully revive one's consciousness and once again live a Krishna-centered existence and attain perfection in all spheres of life.

The Holy Name of Krishna will illumine one's heart and empower one with Krishna shakti (energy). One will have realization of one's true nature, that is, one is not a material body but is actually a spirit soul and part and parcel of Krishna. One will enjoy being in the material world, but from the vantage point of knowledge (*jnana*) renunciation (*vairagya*) and devotion (bhakti). One will know one's actual nature is in devotion and act as such. One lives a liberated life which is real living. There is no more anxiety, fear, stress or negative emotions which burn up true happiness; only a peaceful, happy and harmonious existence, which is an extension of Vrindavana life.

When one lives a harmonious life of Krishna bhakti or Krishna sharanam, one becomes dear to Krishna. Surrender (*sharanam*) means to depend on Krishna in all aspects of life. Lord Krishna oversees the life of His devotees. A devotee is completely taken care of by Krishna. Like Arjuna, one will know, their illusion will be gone and they will be ready to do as Krishna says (*"nasto mohah smrtir labdha ... karisye vacanam tava"*—BG 18.73). No more following our own will. Lord Krishna instructed us to surrender to Him. Surrendering to Krishna is not passive, but requires actively dovetailing our consciousness with the Supreme consciousness and acting accordingly.

One should be fully loyal to Krishna as He is the Supreme Predominator and well-wisher. Living entities are subordinates, as a child is fully dependant on their mother. If one tries to act independently one will invariably make mistakes, because one lacks knowledge and one's senses are imperfect. Also, one's ego is guided by desire (*kama*) which will guide one in the wrong direction. If one rides a bike at 10 miles an hour and then holds onto a car, the bike will travel at the speed of the car without any effort, as one who dovetails one's consciousness with Krishna's will similarly effortlessly speed ahead. Therefore, the best way is to act remembering Krishna ("*mām anusmara yudhya ca*"—BG 8.7). Krishna as the Supersoul will guide one from within.

Every moment of one's life, one should keep Krishna or God in the center. One should just remember Krishna with love and devotion. This will make one's life perfect and happy. Remembering Krishna infuses one with the qualities of Krishna ("*sarvair guṇais tatra samāsate surāḥ*"—SB 5.18.12). Especially when one chants, one becomes electrified or Krishnized. One becomes truthful, compassionate, forgiving, satisfied, grateful, humble, free and detached, full of knowledge and feels loving empathy towards all living beings and everything. Krishna is the reservoir of all transcendental qualities, and by tuning into Krishna consciousness, one becomes infused with these qualities.

Human life is meant for developing Krishna consciousness; that is one's real duty. One must find the meaning of life. Who are we? Who is God? Where are we going? Sri Sanatana and Sri Rupa Goswami were government ministers, highly educated and very wealthy. However, they felt that their lives were meaningless and painful. Sanatana Goswami asked Sri Chaitanya Mahaprabhu (CC Madhya 20.102), *"Ke ami, kene amaya, jare tapa-traya?"* (Who am I? Why do I suffer the threefold miseries?) Mahaprabhu bestowed mercy on them, and they went on to become *acaryas* (religious leaders) and proponents of Gaudia Vaishnavism. Lord Chaitanya made the process simple; just chant the Holy Name of Krishna, live a pure life and be victorious (*"Param vijayate Sri Krishna sankirtanam"*—*Shikshashtakam*).

If one pleases Krishna by one's actions, then Lord Krishna will also please one. When one feeds the stomach, then the stomach energizes the entire body. When one waters the root of a tree, then all the leaves and branches are refreshed. Similarly, by serving Krishna and following His instructions, one becomes successful and happy. One attains *dharma, artha, kama, moksha* ... everything. Life becomes a song: enchanting, knowledgeable and blissful.

However, one cannot worship Krishna properly without being freed from material contaminations, because one will be under Maya (the personification of material energy) or the three modes of material nature. One therefore chants the Holy Names to purify oneself. One should also study *The Bhagavad Gita* and other *shastras*. Without knowledge, one's understanding will be superficial and one's faith (*shraddha*) will be weak. Knowledge leads one to perfection of self-realization. By knowledge one can see oneself as one is: Brahman or pure eternal existence. By knowledge, one realizes that one is not the body, but the indwelling spirit soul.

Gradually, one can fix one's mind on Krishna's lotus feet and be surcharged with Krishna's energy. Remembering Krishna's pastimes and Holy Name will transform one's life. One's existence and everything around one becomes transcendental. One becomes full of knowledge, full of happiness and a fully surrendered servitor of Krishna. One may be physically in the material world, but in truth, one experiences Goloka Vrindavana life while here on earth.

The spiritual knowledge one acquires is never lost. As per *The Bhagavad Gita*, the topmost knowledge is Krishna consciousness (it is *raja vidya*, or royal knowledge), that is, one is not the body, but a soul and Lord Krishna is the Supreme Soul (Paramatma). As a part and parcel of Krishna, one should tune in with the Supersoul. All other knowledge is subordinate to *Brahma vidya*, that is, when one knows Krishna, one becomes the knower of everything. Not only spiritual knowledge, but also material knowledge, such as science, arts and medicine is also retained as essence in the soul. When one reincarnates, the talent of prodigies is manifested from their previous life. The preferences, talents and knowledge of a person are indications of their previous life's experiences. Lord Krishna says that there is no loss or diminution of one's spiritual gain (BG 2.40). If one is Krishna conscious and lives a *sattvic* life, one may continue one's progress even on a higher planet like those of Brahma, Chandra or Varuna. One may eventually go to Goloka Vrindavana, the place from which, having once gone, one never returns (BG 15.3–4).

In ordinary consciousness one is sure to make mistakes. In Krishna consciousness all one's actions and decisions will be correct. One's guidance and inspirations will come from the Supersoul. In super consciousness one's mind is absorbed in the pure self. When the pure self is linked to the Supersoul by bhakti, one attains super consciousness. A devotee becomes infallible. Whatever one says will come to pass and whatever one does will be correct. Krishna consciousness is pure undifferentiated consciousness and there is no duality. Therefore, all problems are solved, as one is infallible in Krishna consciousness.

Krishna consciousness brings Krishna into one's heart and makes one's life enjoyable because Krishna is the ocean of pleasure ("*ananda-cinmaya-rasa*"—*Brahma Samhita* 5.37). One feels happy and content. Whatever one does, becomes successful by itself, because there is no possibility of error. When one thinks of Krishna, one is under Krishna's spiritual potency (*daivi-prakriti*). In Krishna consciousness one is in one's natural state. Whenever one is in material consciousness, one is anxious being under the ploy of the three modes of material nature (goodness, passion, ignorance) or *gunas* (*sattva, raja, tama*), and the threefold miseries of the material world, namely *adhyatmic* (miseries of the mind and body), *adhi-bhautic* (miseries caused by other living entities) and *adhi-daivic* (natural calamities). The material world is an illusion where people are prone to cheating, and with their imperfect senses they are sure to make mistakes.

But when one is in Krishna consciousness, one is untouched by the *gunas*. One becomes enlightened and joyful. Bhakti yoga is all auspicious (*Shivada*). It uproots the threefold miseries from one's life. Krishna consciousness solves all one's problems, gives one peace and happiness and makes one's life fully successful. One abides in a happy eternal state of bliss and knowledge of God.

To execute Krishna consciousness, one has to do four activities, namely chanting the Holy Names, only eating *prasadam*, hearing and reading Krishna katha (stories of Krishna), and performing deity worship. These four activities will make one's life successful. It's hardly difficult. This will please Krishna, and Krishna will also please His devotee. One will be blissful. This way, one will always remember Krishna and one's body, mind and speech will be Krishnized. One's whole existence will be pure. One should be mindful of one's physical, emotional and mental wellbeing. Without harmonious wellbeing, Krishna consciousness does not take place.

To progress on the spiritual path, one must speak the truth and live the truth. One should always work in pure consciousness. One should view all living entities as siblings, because Krishna or God is the seed-giving Father. All beings are part and parcel of God. Thus, if one follows the principles of truth, nonviolence, and empathy, and practices mantra meditation of Krishna Nama, one will succeed for sure. Krishna as the Supersoul in all of us will guide us through this *samsara* (the material world). One need not fear.

Living entities are simultaneously material and spiritual beings. One's body, mind, intelligence, and ego are material, but one's soul is spiritual. One's body is temporary, and so is one's material nature. However, one's soul is eternal in its original condition and it is full of knowledge and bliss (*sat cit ananda*), as is Krishna.

So if one wishes to be happy and blissful, one must reduce one's material attachment. By following the bhakti path, that is, by hearing, chanting, remembering and worshipping Krishna, one can be situated in one's spiritual nature or Krishna consciousness.

Krishna consciousness is mindful absorption in Krishna. One is always aware of Lord Krishna and feels His presence. Lord Krishna instructed the *gopis* (milkmaids of Vrindavana) that everything is His energy. God and His energies are inconceivably, simultaneously one. Therefore when one sees the sky, trees, animals and plants, feels a cool breeze, or tastes water or a delicious fruit, then one should feel the presence of Krishna. When one is in remembrance of Krishna, one is with Him.

On the spiritual path one must be very disciplined. One must follow the regulative principles seriously. For example, if one eats non-vegetarian food, one's spiritual progress will be immediately arrested. One must observe *tapa* (austerity), *saucha* (cleanliness), *daya* (compassion) and *satyam* (truth) which are the four limbs of *dharma*. One must therefore avoid *striya* (lust and illicit sex), *suna* (flesh eating), *pana* (intoxication), and *dyuta* (gambling and cheating). One should instead be clean and fresh, which will put one in *sattva guna*, chant the Holy Names which will purify the mind, worship Sri Radha Madhava (Krishna) which will develop a personal relationship with Him, develop *jnana* to realize that we are spirit soul and God's servant, and cultivate *vairagya* which will result in detachment from material nature and lust.

These processes allow one to know Krishna in truth. When one is fully absorbed in thoughts of Krishna (His name, fame, form, and pastimes), then one is Krishna conscious. When one chants the Holy Names, then one is also in touch with Krishna. Krishna consciousness can happen gradually or in an instant. Depending on one's sincerity and *sadhana*, one may spontaneously transition from material consciousness to Krishna consciousness all of a sudden. Also, depending on one's *guna* and *karma*, one may take a longer time. Krishna's qualities manifest spontaneously as one makes progress in Krishna consciousness. All of a sudden one's life can become sublime and Krishnized. One becomes capable of astonishing feats, and can become a teacher of Krishna consciousness in this state.

If one follows Lord Sri Krishna's instructions in *The Bhagavad Gita*, all one's endeavours will be successful and one will be happy. If one does not follow His instructions, all one's endeavours will be ruined (*"viddhi nastan acetasah"* —BG 3.32). One's knowledge and vision are imperfect. Therefore, one is bound to make mistakes. One should live one's life in Krishna consciousness, tuning one's consciousness to the Supreme consciousness (*"yoga-sthah kuru karmani"* — BG 2.48). Then one will make no mistakes because one will be in pure consciousness or connected with the Absolute Truth, Krishna. Even if one does make mistakes, Lord Krishna will take care of it. As He says (BG 18.66), *"mam ekam saranam vraja"* (just surrender unto Me). Be in a surrendered mood, as Arjuna was. Do not do things or plan things on your own; be an instrument (*nimitta*) of God's plan. Devotees should allow God's work to be accomplished through them.

Being in Krishna consciousness is the most joyful condition. Prahlad Maharaj told his friends, "let us chant Krishna's name and be in Krishna consciousness." His friends wanted to play games and be happy. But Prahlad Maharaj told them that being in Krishna consciousness is the highest enjoyment. Material enjoyment is temporary and mixed with pain and suffering. Spiritual enjoyment is eternal and pure. Material enjoyment makes one weary, but spiritual enjoyment is ever refreshing.

In childhood, when one begins one's spiritual education, one is a *brahmachari* or *brahmacharini*. *Brahmacharya* means conduct leading to Brahma or Krishna. It is better to get spiritual training early, otherwise one gets materially entangled and deviates from the path of upliftment. If one misses the opportunity in childhood, one should nevertheless start to live a pure life and chant the Holy Names immediately. As Confucian scholar Issai Sato said, "One who studies in youth will accomplish things in maturity. One who studies in maturity will not become feeble in old age."

If a child practices Krishna consciousness, he will make fewer mistakes in life and he will be healthy, wealthy, wise and blissful. Do not delay spiritual training; the earlier one starts the better it is ("*kaumāraṁ ācaret prajño*"—SB 7.6.1). A Krishna conscious person lives a thrilling, deep life. A devotee's mind is clear, sharp and lucid; one is patient, humble, and kind. A devotee is truthful, forgiving, and helpful without envy or judgement. He clutches onto Krishna's lotus feet and never lets go ("*gurunapi vicalyate*"—BG 6.20–23).

A Krishna conscious person is always absorbed in Krishna, but not distracted from daily activities. One goes about one's daily business attentively and expertly: eating, sleeping, working, chanting, and divinely loving; the devotee always remembers Krishna (*God! God! God!* by Paramahansa Yogananda). Like a fish in water or a bird in the sky, a devotee is effortlessly immersed in Krishna thoughts and is in the present moment, not thinking of the past or future, without anxiety. *Shikshashtakam* says "... *kirtaniyah sada harihi,*" which is that "in such a (humble) state of mind, one can chant the Holy Name constantly." Thinking of the form of Krishna, one is sure to attain Him (*"mam anusmara yuddhya ca"*—BG 8.7). Krishna is always present in a devotee's mind.

The goal of human life is Krishna or God (*"athato Brahma jijnasa"*—the first aphorism in the Vedanta). Never lose that focus. Steady your mind by Krishna consciousness and do not allow yourself to fall under the sway of material nature. One may have health, wealth, and knowledge of philosophy and science, but without Krishna, happiness will be elusive. If one succeeds in Krishna consciousness, one will have everything because one will be Krishnized. Krishna has all the opulences. When one becomes Krishnized, one acquires Krishna's attributes. A devotee manifests these qualities more and more with advancement in Krishna consciousness.

By surrendering to Krishna, the devotee becomes sinless because Lord Krishna frees one from all sins (*"aham tvam sarva-papebhyo, mokshayishami, ma sucah"*—BG 18.66). One then lives only in the orb of Krishna's mercy and protection. One does all one's activities dovetailing to Krishna in *yukta vairagya* (detachment in union with God). A devotee works on the material plane, but offers the fruits of action to Krishna. Thus, one is a true renouncer. Work done in devotion is superior to simply renouncing work.

If one wants to engage in devotional service, one has to be sinless. A sinful person is always restless and therefore cannot engage in chanting or in Krishna consciousness. One has to clean up one's body, mind, and intellect (ego). One's body is a *kshetra* or field. One must cultivate this field in the service of Krishna like King Ambarisha. He used all his senses to worship Krishna. King Ambarisha used his hands to perform *arati*, his tongue to taste *prasadam* and chant Krishna's name, his eyes to behold the deity of Krishna, his sense of smell for flowers and incense offered to Krishna, and with his ears, he listened to stories about Krishna (Krishna katha). Similarly, by only allowing activities of the body to be used in devotion to Krishna (bhakti), all one's activities will be favourable for Krishna consciousness (*"Hrisikesha Hrisikena-sevanam bhaktir ucyate"* —CC Madhya 19.170).

It is important to study books written by pure devotees of Krishna or *acaryas*. In this way one cultivates one's spiritual potencies. Knowledge of Krishna destroys nescience (*tamasa*) and thus one becomes enlightened. Such *acaryas*, who are true representatives of Krishna, transmit actual knowledge of Krishna through their writing or literary works. These *mahajans* are true gurus because they do not mask the original message with their own interpretation. *Mahajans* means "great people"— *maha* means "great" and *jan* means "people" (as related to "*les gens*" in French and "gents" in English). These people present transcendental knowledge of Krishna as it is. Knowers of Krishna *tattva* or the science of Krishna are true gurus, *acaryas*, and *mahajans* ("*yei kṛṣṇa-tattva-vettā, sei guru haya*"—CC Madhya 8.128). Simply by knowing the science of Krishna, one attains liberation and becomes successful. Follow in the footsteps of the *mahajans* and associate with them through their *vanis* or sayings and writings. Such association empowers one towards rapid enlightenment. Confucius said that one can become wise by reflection, imitation or experience. In Krishna consciousness, one can follow all three.

One's human body goes through many changes throughout one's lifetime. A baby's body is totally different than that of a youth. The same is true for a youthful body compared to an old body. The bodily transformation occurs not only outwardly, but also at the cellular level. Every few years, we have new sets of cells as old cells die out. In other words, we go through a series of reincarnations throughout our lifetime. However, one's consciousness does not change. This consciousness is experienced by one's actual self or soul. The soul powers one's body because it is a form of energy which is never destroyed. When the soul resides in the body, the body is alive. When the body is dead, the soul goes to some other planet in the universe. The soul, depending on its karma, may or may not take another body again.

Do not be afraid of death. Death frees one from bodily consciousness. One's body, or ego, is the source of all one's miseries. For a devotee, one's *svarupa* or constitutional position is revealed at the time of death, which is eternal knowledge and bliss. Thus for a Krishna conscious person, death is the point of liberation when one is fully engrossed in love of Krishna, when the devotee journeys to Krishna Loka.

Rabindranath Tagore wrote that *"tuhu mama shyam saman"*: death is like Shyam. (Shyam is another name of Krishna meaning deep, green-blue. Thailand, once called Siam, was named after Krishna for its lushness.) *The Bhagavad Gita* (10.34) also says Krishna is all-devouring death (*"mrtyuh sarva-haras caham"*). For a devotee, death is only disappearance from the material world and elevation to Krishna Loka (Goloka Vrindavana). If one thinks this way, one will have more knowledge about actual life, more detachment from the material world, and consequently, more attachment to God or Krishna.

Fortunate is the person who asks the questions: Who am I? Who is God? Where am I going? What is the goal of life? More fortunate is one who understands that one is not the body (or ego), but the spirit soul and a part and parcel of God. And most fortunate is one who becomes a devotee of Krishna as a result of knowing this.

Process

A *bhakta* (devotee of Krishna) should be a *jnani*, a *karmi*, and a *dhyani* at the same time. If one practices bhakti one's Krishna consciousness will grow. If one does material work (karma) in relation to Krishna, one will advance in Krishna consciousness too because one is working for Krishna. If one studies spiritual subjects (*dhyana*) to further Krishna consciousness, one's conviction and faith will grow. If one studies material subjects, such as philosophy, arts or science in relation to Krishna, one will have new insights into Krishna consciousness and will be able to integrate them into one's life. Meditation on Krishna's name and form will also increase one's love for Krishna. Love of Krishna is the pang of separation one feels when one doesn't see the deity or read about Krishna. One must know about Krishna by regularly reading as much as possible from *The Bhagavad Gita*, *Srimad Bhagavatam* and *Sri Chaitanya Charitamrita*, otherwise one's bhakti will not grow strong or mature. Sri Chaitanya Mahaprabhu said that one should not be lazy to study *siddhanta* (philosophy), as one's mind becomes clear and any doubts are removed.

Once an old *brahmana* came to see Lord Buddha and asked Him:

"How are You a Buddha, The Enlightened One?"

The Buddha answered:

"What has to be known, I have known. What has to be abandoned, I have abandoned. What has to be developed, I have developed, therefore, Oh *brahmana*, I am a Buddha."

An enlightened person has total clarity about life and the world. They are free from hate, anger, and desire. They are peaceful and mindfully develop transcendental consciousness or Krishna consciousness. A devotee is also *stitha prajna* (of steady wisdom), desireless, fully satisfied in Krishna consciousness and unshaken in adversity. They are undisturbed by good and evil, and have complete self-control. In this way, they are tranquil and established in the *Brahmi sthiti* state. What has to be known is that one is not the body, but the spirit soul, what has to be abandoned is material consciousness as well as core-destroying tendencies such as hate, anger, jealousy, lust and greed. What has to be developed is Krishna consciousness.

The soul is naturally inclined to love Krishna, the Supersoul, because the soul is born of Krishna. It is how a child loves the mother without being taught. The child feels great happiness in the mother's lap. Similarly, the soul is happy being with the Supersoul.

If a child's parents are rich and educated, then they're happy to see their child growing up nicely. The parents don't have any other expectation. In the same way, our Supreme Parent, Krishna, who has everything and needs nothing, is pleased when His children (the living entities) live nicely and love Him, becoming a part of His household (*Krishnera samsara*). One can attain one's original blissful state by loving Krishna.

Whatever activities one does—reading, writing, cooking, cleaning, eating, sleeping, working—one should dovetail one's mind with Krishna. In this way one will always be with Krishna like the *gopis* of Vrindavana, who always thought of Krishna. With Krishna in mind, everything one does will be an offering (*yajna*) to Vishnu, or Krishna. One won't have to make a separate endeavour. Eating *prasadam* (food offered to Krishna) keeps our consciousness in an elevated state. We become Krishnized by eating food offered to Krishna. If possible, one should eat only *prasadam*; it is a way to infuse ourselves with Krishna shakti (power of Krishna) as a piece of wire gets electrified when an electrical current passes through it. We can go about our daily business with spiritualized enthusiasm. Offering incense, lights and flowers also spiritualizes our senses and consciousness. Our homes become purified like a temple; by worshipping Krishna, we create mini Vrindavanas. With elevated consciousness, our body, mind, intelligence and the world around us function on a spiritual plane.

One should engage all one's senses in the service of Lord Krishna, like Maharaja Ambarisha did. In this way, one becomes purified of material contamination and becomes pure and spiritual. One should take deity *darshan*, smell the flowers offered to the deities, read from *The Bhagavad Gita* and eat *prasadam*. Chanting of the Harinam and partaking of the *prasadam* are very important because this process quickly brings our senses under control. Gradually one becomes *dhira* or grounded by spiritual practices. One's mind and intellect becomes fixed at the lotus feet of Sri Krishna. One then does not waver from that position. One's original Krishna consciousness awakens as the dust of material contamination is removed from the mirror of one's heart. One becomes a *bhakta* (devotee of Krishna). One becomes perfect and fully successful.

By reading books like *The Bhagavad Gita* and *The Sri Chaitanya Charitamrita* our consciousness becomes transcendental. Meditation on the content of these books lifts our consciousness from the mundane, physical, mental and intellectual level to pure Krishna consciousness. When we meditate on the content of these books, our negative emotions such as shame, guilt, anger and fear are replaced with courage, enthusiasm and happiness. We understand that we are not physical bodies but spirit souls and there is an all-encompassing ultimate reality, Vāsudeva Krishna, both physical and spiritual. The power that binds the whole universe, the living entities and the cosmos, is pure Love (God). Studying kindles the fire of knowledge in our hearts. As Prabhupada said, the words of *The Gita* are sufficient to give us enlightenment. Krishna consciousness is pure undifferentiated consciousness from which all living entities and the material manifestations emanate (BG 10.8).

All our activities should be performed in relation to Krishna (Krishna samsara). Whatever we eat, whatever job we do, whatever austerity (*tapa*) we perform, we should do those thinking of Krishna (*mac-citta mat para man mana*). This is easily accomplished when we think that we are living in Krishna's household. We prepare food for Krishna, we go to work and earn money to maintain Krishna's house and we study so that we can understand Krishna. Everything belongs to Krishna: "*isa vasyam idam sarvam*"—*Isopanishad*, mantra 1. Krishna is our real master (employer), maintainer, protector and friend. Krishna is the real doer; we are His subordinates. When our activity is in tune with His divine plan our lives become joyful. When Krishna is pleased with us, we become inundated with happiness. Conversely, when we become inundated with happiness, we know we have pleased Krishna.

One should live one's daily life in an attitude of love and gratitude to God. Knowledge, wealth, health, whatever one has, one obtained by Krishna's mercy, otherwise how would one get it? *Sri Isopanishad* says "*isa vashya idam sarvam*," everything belongs to God. One could easily be poor, sick and ignorant. One could even be dead. Therefore, be grateful to Krishna for everything. Also, be compassionate to other living entities, trees and animals, because they are Krishna's part and parcel, like you. In this age, by chanting the Holy Names and being merciful to other living entities one can realize God (*"jīve doyā, kṛṣṇa-nām, sarva-dharma-sār"*—*Nadiyah Godrume Nityananda Mahajana*, a song by Bhaktivinoda Thakura). Gratitude and compassion will open one's heart, elevate one to a higher consciousness and make one a perfect devotee.

By regular studies of *The Bhagavad Gita* and other scriptures, one's understanding about Krishna, the soul, material nature and the spiritual world becomes deeper. The study of transcendental literature burns up karma. Acquiring knowledge by studying is essential to be enlightened or Krishna conscious. By transmission of pure knowledge of Krishna, Lord Krishna awakens the seed of love in one's heart as He did for the sun god Vivasvan, or Prince Arjuna. The writings of the *acaryas* facilitate the transmission of this *Brahma-jnana* (Krishna consciousness). *Acaryas* such as Rupa and Sanatana Goswami, Narottama Das Thakur, Bhaktivinoda Thakur, and recently, Srila Prabhupada are our gurus of the present time. Lord Krishna is the original Guru because He gave this

Brahma-jnana to the sun god millions of years ago. What is this *Brahma-jnana*? It is the knowledge that one is not the body, but spirit soul, a part and parcel of Krishna, and thus one's duty is to serve Krishna. One is happy and joyful serving Krishna.

To understand Krishna, one must first be self-realized (*Brahma bhuta*). One's body, mind and intelligence are underpinned by pure unborn, eternal existence, or Brahman. The underling existence of the cosmos is Parabrahman or the *sat* aspect of the Absolute Truth. Brahman is inactive, and a devotee realizing this aspect experiences pure peace. Brahman pervading the body of a *jiva* is *atman* and self-conscious.

Parabrahman pervading the entire cosmos is Paramatma and conscious of the entire cosmos. The Paramatma controls and regulates the entire cosmos, including all living entities, the whole material nature and atoms. The Paramatma resides in the heart of all living entities (*antar yami*) along with the soul, or *atman*. Paramatma is the *cit* or the knowledge aspect of the Absolute Truth. Paramatma is all knowing, and a devotee understanding the Paramatma or Supersoul is creative, knowledgeable and has a great understanding of the world. The devotee who understands Brahman has peace, and the devotee who understands Paramatma has peace and joy.

The Absolute Truth with *sat* and *cit* is also a person, and is Krishna or Bhagavan. As we are persons, so is Lord Krishna a person. Krishna is *sat cit ananda vigraha* or the embodiment of eternal existence, all knowing and blissful. Lord Krishna plays with His Radha Rani and

His cowherd boys and girls, and holds His flute in His hands. A devotee knowing Krishna is full of knowledge and bliss, exhibits all opulences of Krishna and is eternally devoted to Him. If a devotee realizes Brahman or Paramatma and does not engage in devotional service, then the devotee risks falling down or losing spiritual gains.

If one becomes Krishna's devotee, He will provide one with all one's needs. After all, He provides for all other living entities. A devotee is however, specially favoured, because a devotee approaches Krishna. As one gets the warmth of the sun when one goes outside, so does a devotee get the benediction of Krishna when he approaches Krishna. Krishna's mercy, like the sun, is available to all living entities, if one but approaches Him. By devotional service a *bhakta* gradually becomes like Krishna (in quality) and becomes Krishnized. One thus acquires the six opulences of the Lord, namely wealth (*aisvarya*), strength (*virya*), fame (*yasha*), beauty (*sriya*), knowledge (*jnana*), and renunciation (*vairagya*). A devotee attains all the perfections and all the successes; he is beyond the four material conditions of birth (*janma*), death (*mrityu*), old age (*jara*) and disease (*vyadhi*).

Everything in this world is temporary, unreliable and uncertain. Therefore, one is constantly assailed by anxiety, worry and fear. The only way to overcome these anxieties, fears and doubts is to anchor oneself to the Absolute Truth (*Satyam Param*), which is permanent, reliable and certain.

The Absolute Truth is also a person, Bhagavan, full of love and mercy. We could not be persons if God were not a person. God cannot be less than us. When one understands that one is not the body, but the spirit soul and part and parcel of Krishna, all one's anxieties, worries and fear vanish. Anxieties, worries and fear are related to one's material body. Truth is permanent; it is related to the soul. When one speaks the truth and lives the truth, one is in one's true nature and in touch with the Absolute Truth or Krishna.

To make one's life happy and successful, one must practice austerity or *tapasya* (*tapo divyam*). *Tapasya* means self-controlled conduct in divine consciousness. Practicing *tapasya* leads to transcendental life. Obey *shastra*, be respectful to parents and teachers, be content and grateful, and speak truthfully. Never stop learning, be it material or spiritual knowledge. All one's activities should be performed being absorbed in the thought of Krishna (Krishna consciousness). To love Krishna, serve Krishna and please Krishna spontaneously with a pure heart is one's ultimate goal of life on earth. One's real business is to revive one's relationship to Krishna. Krishna is our *pita* (father), *mata* (mother), *dhata* (maintainer), *pitamaha* (grandfather or ancestor) and most beloved. One must realize that one's relationship with Krishna is very close and deep; one's relationship with Him is as close as can be, like a mother and newborn child.

Self-control builds one's character and one's moral fiber. One's mind becomes strong and wise. Self-control elevates one from *tama* and *raja gunas* to the platform of *sattva guna*, and thus makes one steady. One's *shraddha* (faith) becomes unwavering. One becomes energized by devotional service and also becomes healthy, fit and wise.

As faith grows on one's spiritual path, Krishna gives intelligence (*buddhi*). Krishna consciousness is for the intelligent. Foolish people cannot understand the subtle concepts, such as the soul, God, piety, sin, karma, *jnana*, etc. *Buddhi* means power to analyze things with a proper perspective. At best, fools (*mudhas*) can understand things in relation to their body, such as pain and suffering. For meat eaters, even this is difficult, because their brain becomes dull and their mind becomes insensitive. Bhakti does not awaken in the minds of such people. God is all merciful and a devotee is godly. She or he has Krishna's qualities.

Cruel people, like meat eaters and hunters, cannot become devotees because compassion does not arise in their hearts. They disobey the principle of *ahimsa* by killing other living entities who are also part and parcel of Krishna; therefore, they cannot realize God. Also, those people who are attached to their senses and are greedy for wealth and material enjoyment do not seek God because such thoughts do not come to their minds. It is beyond them to grasp spiritual truths. Therefore, one must undergo *tapasya* (penance) and live a simple life with high thoughts.

Bhakti or Krishna consciousness means absorption of one's body and mind in Krishna as one offers service to the Lord. Material energy used for sense gratification causes bondage, whereas the same material energy used for the service of Krishna is liberating. The process of bhakti yoga is pleasant even in the initial stages, because one prepares delicious food for Krishna and reads about Krishna, sings, dances and chants for Krishna in the form of the deities. Even if these activities are flawed in the beginning, they slowly become purified, if performed with sincerity.

The chanting of the Holy Names removes all material contamination and conditioning. One becomes situated in one's original nature; one becomes happy and does not regret the past, nor crave an opulent future. There is Krishna and there is the devotee lovingly offering service to Krishna; there is only bliss in Krishna's presence.

As we happily (*susukham*) follow the principle of plain living and high thinking, we gradually free ourselves from *anarthas* (meaningless material contaminations that cause problems or inconveniences in our lives). We understand our true nature (*svarupa*), and our materialism disappears. Our body, mind, and speech become pure. The chanting of the Holy Names bestows upon us numerous spiritual and material benedictions. We become more and more established in Krishna consciousness.

As one performs bhakti yoga one sees that whatever Krishna has said is true, and one's faith grows. One notices events and sometimes what others say to us as direction from Krishna. Seeing results, our faith becomes firm; we are convinced. This stage is *nishta*, fixed. Our heart enjoys hearing and chanting the Holy Names and reading about Lord Krishna's pastimes. Thinking and seeing Krishna in our heart becomes a daily source of inspiration. This taste, *ruci*, is a very tangible stage of bhakti. One truly relishes this state of Krishna consciousness. As we advance further, we become more attached to Krishna and His pastimes, form and attributes. This stage is called *asakti* (or divine addiction). Sometimes tears well up in our eyes thinking of Krishna or seeing the deities (*"premāñjana-cchurita-bhakti-vilocanena"*—*Brahma Samhita* 5.38). This stage is called *bhava*. As we continue with our hearing, chanting and remembering we feel love for Krishna. We hanker to see the deities, hear Krishna lila and enjoy reading *The Srimad Bhagavatam*. This is Krishna *prema*, the culmination of the bhakti process. This is also Vrindavana life. Our life becomes sublime and we live in Krishna's household, Krishnera *samsara*.

Actually, our happiness starts as soon as we start to chant, eat *prasadam*, and hear Krishna katha. Hearing about the Lord's pastimes and activities is by itself a righteous activity. Lord Krishna says that one who studies the conversation between Him and Arjuna worships Him with intelligence, and one who listens becomes free from sinful reaction—BG 18.71–72. Simply by hearing Krishn katha, one understands the Absolute Truth and becomes free: "*śṛṇvatāṁ sva-kathāḥ kṛṣṇaḥ*"—SB 1.2.17.

As we progress, all our problems start to melt away. Lust, greed and envy (*kama*, *lobha*, and *asuya*) diminish and we become happier and happier. Our bodily conception of life decreases; we realize that we are spirit souls, *atman*, and part and parcel of God, the Paramatma (*aham Brahmasmi*). It is our natural duty and pleasant to serve Him, please Him, and love Him. That is perfection of life and true success.

Our life becomes sweet when we start to enjoy spiritual life, which is our real life. We love the Holy Names; we love to hear Krishna katha. We feel happy thinking of Krishna. The blue sky, the expansive waters, the *shyam* forests remind us of Krishna, Shyamasundara. The taste or *ruci* of *Krishna-bhakti-rasa* (the nectar of devotion) is the beginning of the transformation of our material life into devotional life. Until this point our *sadhana* is based on regulations; beyond this point our *sadhana* is spontaneous. We feel deep attraction to Radha Krishna, to Mahaprabhu and everybody and everything related to Krishna. The Holy Name becomes like rolling waves in our mind. As Paramahansa Yogananda said, "life is sweet when Thy song flows through me." *The Bhagavad Gita, The Srimad Bhagavatam* and *The Sri Chaitanya Charitamrita* become nectarean to our ears. Whatever we do—eating, sleeping, working, chanting—our whole existence becomes sweet.

Bhakti is the natural tendency of the soul. A soul cannot but love God, as a child loves the mother. There is no contentment in our heart without reposing our love in Krishna. When we love Krishna, we love everything. We find love and beauty everywhere: in nature, people, in all living entities.

Chant the Holy Names of the Pancha Tattva (Jaya Sri Krishna Chaitanya, Prabhu Nityananda, Sri Advaita, Gadadhara, Srivasadi, Gaura bhakta vrinda) before chanting each round of the Maha Mantra to evoke the mercy of the Pancha Tattva and to make our chanting offenseless. Then chant the Maha Mantra (*Hare Krishna, Hare Krishna, Krishna Krishna, Hare Hare, Hare Rama, Hare Rama, Rama Rama, Hare Hare*) by holding the *japa* beads in the right hand with the beads draped over the middle finger. Move the bead towards oneself with the thumb after each unhurried mindful complete chant of the Maha Mantra. By chanting we come in touch with the spiritual potency of Lord Krishna.

Start the day with *japa yajna* and eat sanctified food (*prasadam*)—BG 3.13. If we take a shower, calm the mind by taking deep breaths and do some yoga postures before chanting, our *japa* meditation will be deeper. Chanting in front of deities is also conducive to deep meditation. By chanting the Holy Names we associate with Krishna, because the Lord's Name and Form are non-different (*Brahma Samhita* 5.1). One should not worry too much about offenses (*aparadha*); gradually our chanting will become pure (*shuddha nama*). After completing the *japa*, one may sit for a few minutes, feel grateful and enjoy the calmness of the mind. One's experience will be pleasurable and lasting. By chanting the Holy Names we come in touch with the superior energy of Lord Krishna. We become suffused with Krishna's energy and we perform our daily activities with enthusiasm and happiness, and make decisions that are in tune with the cosmos.

After *japa*, our memory of our actual self is revived; that is that we are spirit souls and not the body. We understand that God is our Eternal Parent; we are part and parcel of Krishna. It is our duty and pleasure to be a servitor of Krishna. That is our *svarupa* or true state. Service to Lord Krishna is filled with bliss, and not like serving in our material world, which is filled with sorrow. The more we chant the Maha Mantra, the more we live in soul consciousness and less in body consciousness. Gradually we will live constantly in soul consciousness.

The superior energy of the Lord moves the entire universe as our soul (*atma*) moves our body. The *atma* is tiny, or "atomic." The Paramatma or Supersoul is infinite. Otherwise, what would be present beyond the limit of the material world? God pervades the entire material world and beyond. Therefore God is infinite or unlimited. God is omnipresent, present everywhere.

If we wish to experience "unlimited life," or continued happiness, knowledge and truth, we must be Krishna conscious. By chanting the Holy Names, we remove all our blocks to spiritual progress. By dovetailing our consciousness to Krishna, we open the door of unlimited happiness, full of wealth, strength, fame, beauty, knowledge, and renunciation. Once we attain the state of yoga or Krishna consciousness, we never fall from Krishna's presence.

In his famous chiasmus, poet John Keats said that "Beauty is truth, truth beauty." Beauty is the most attractive opulence of Lord Krishna; everyone is attracted to beauty. Because truth exists, therefore God exists. God is the Absolute Truth or ultimate existence. For example, we exist, matter or energy exists, and natural mathematical laws exist. As our existence is underpinned by these truths, so is the existence of God, the Ultimate Person. The Ultimate Primordial Person or God is Krishna. Truth pervades the entire cosmos, therefore the cosmos exists. Therefore, Krishna is omnipresent (present everywhere), omniscient (all knowing), omnipotent (most powerful) and eternal. Krishna is fully related to the entire cosmos and all entities in it, living or nonliving.

Krishna incarnates anywhere in the universe, whenever there is a discrepancy in His cosmic order, Sanatana Dharma. He always protects His devotees and innocent living entities, and destroys the miscreants. Krishna also enjoys the love and affection of His devotees. When one lives one's life being conscious of God, there are no difficulties. But when one lives through one's false ego, problems arise. Problems arise because one does not know one's true nature and thus lives in the mode of ignorance, behaving erratically. One is out of tune with the Absolute Truth.

When we dovetail our consciousness to Krishna consciousness and are always mindful of Krishna, we live in Him. In God we live, move, and have our being (Taittiriya Upanishad). We are in Vrindavana and in Krishna's presence. We sing the name of Krishna. We hear the glories of Krishna. We partake of food offered to Krishna. Our life becomes Krishnized. We become ecstatic. We become inundated with joy.

Krishna consciousness is the utmost necessity for a successful life because it is our normal healthy consciousness. Without it, life is a maze with a myriad of problems, because our body and mind are under the spell of Maya or the three *gunas*. Life is sometimes nice, sometimes miserable. But if we are in Krishna consciousness, we are in touch with the Absolute Truth. We immediately transcend Maya or the three *gunas*, and all our problems are solved (*"sa gunan *samatityaitan"*—BG 14.26). In Krishna consciousness, Lord Krishna guides our lives. There is no possibility of error.

As soon as one wakes up, one should brush one's teeth, clean oneself, chant 16 rounds, and meditate for a few minutes. During the day, listen to *kirtan*, *The Bhagavad Gita*, and Srila Prabhupada's talks. Offer incense, light, water and flowers (as many as possible, more in spring and summer) to Krishna. One should eat only *prasadam*: rice, lentil, fruits, vegetables, milk, cheese, nuts, and grains. Everything should be offered to Krishna.

During the day anything nice and beautiful, such as the blue sky, green vegetation, even the taste of water should remind one of Krishna. One should depend on Krishna, be grateful to Krishna, and love Krishna. This way one can keep oneself in Krishna consciousness all the time and feel His presence. If one keeps oneself in *sattva guna* and chants, one feels happy and one is naturally in a higher consciousness. One feels devotion for Krishna, one feels loved, and one is under *daivi-prakriti* or Yogamaya (God's divine energy). One's heart is satisfied in Krishna consciousness. God gives one the intelligence to see Him everywhere. One is under the deep blue sky bathed in the golden warm sun. One just is, living in the moment, just there under the affectionate gaze of Krishna.

Krishna consciousness is attained by sincerity. One may be very intelligent, one may try hard, but if one is not sincere, one won't succeed. One should make every effort to attain Krishna, God, in this life, because to reincarnate again is risky and one may not even get a human birth, let alone be fortunate enough to be born in conditions conducive to Krishna consciousness ("*sada tad-bhava-bhavita*"—BG 8.6).

Krishna consciousness is a life of higher consciousness. In ordinary consciousness, one is angry, jealous, unkind and dull. In this ordinary condition, one is bothered by even small things, such as the weather (extreme cold and heat), a delayed bus, or a traffic jam. In Krishna consciousness the annoyance over these things is absent. One knows that these things are temporary. In the end, everything will be alright. In Krishna consciousness one is in loving awareness of Krishna, and one is friendly, kind, and one's mind is sharp.

The senses are unruly; they don't allow one to be Krishna conscious. The best way to focus one's mind on Krishna is by using the senses in the service of Krishna, as said in the *Narada Pancharatra* and quoted in *The Chaitanya Charitamrita* (CC Madhya 19.170), "*Hrisikesha Hrisikena-sevanam bhaktir ucyate.*" One can use the tongue to eat *prasadam* and chant the Holy Names. One can smell flowers and incense offered to Krishna. One can listen to talks about Krishna, and songs about Krishna. One can visit temples, take deity *darshan*, and offer obeisance. By engaging our body, mind and words in devotional service, one can purify one's existence and become fit to see Krishna. As Prabhupada says, one has to become fire to enter fire. We have to become pure to be with the Supreme Pure (*pavitra*). By performing *tapasya*, some voluntary restrictions, one can purify oneself and by chanting the Holy Names one can become

Krishnized or Krishna conscious. In *The Bhagavad Gita*, Lord Krishna says that the senses are higher than matter, the mind is higher than the senses, the intelligence is higher than the mind, and the soul is higher than the intelligence.

If one is determined and makes up one's mind to be successful, to attain perfection, one can use the mind and intelligence to make the soul, *atman*, take charge of one's life by the process of bhakti yoga. The soul, being a part and parcel of the Absolute Truth, does not make any mistakes. By chanting the Holy Names one comes to that error-free state. By becoming Krishna conscious, one's soul becomes the controller of one's intelligence, mind and senses.

By following the nine processes of bhakti: hearing, chanting, remembering, deity worship and by partaking *prasadam*, one gradually becomes pure and sinless. One gets the nectarean taste of bhakti. One becomes absorbed in eternity, knowledge, and bliss (*sat cit ananda*). One's soul finds repose in Krishna, and one become supremely satisfied. *Brahmana pathi* is the path of transcendence through knowing oneself as *atman*, which is a part of Brahman, Paramatma and Bhagavan, as described in *The Bhagavad Gita*.

One should gradually develop faith in Krishna by reading *The Bhagavad Gita*. Whatever Krishna has said, whatever instructions He has given, are all true (*"sarvam etad rtam manye yan mam vadasi kesava"* — BG 10.14). If one lives one's life with deep *shraddha* or faith in Krishna and His *lila* (pastimes), and follows His advice, one can live a happy life on earth and at the end of one's life one can be with Him in Goloka Vrindavana (*nitya lila pravishta*, or a partaker of eternal pastimes of Their Lordships Radha and Krishna). One should examine one's mind to see the prime motive that drives one. If it is anything but Krishna, one should replace it; that will guarantee one a successful life.

In one's life, one has many goals and aspirations. However, the ultimate goal should be Krishna. Do everything, but in yoga or Krishna consciousness (*"yoga-sthah kuru karmani"*—BG 2.48). While seeking enlightenment, one chops wood and carries water, and after enlightenment, one also chops wood and carries water. Although outwardly one does the same tasks, one's consciousness has changed from material to spiritual. Don't neglect material work for spiritual work. While doing worldly things, the Krishna conscious person's mind is on Krishna. Work for Krishna. Paramahansa Yogananda said *Krishna is the real employer, maintain your home (Krishna owns the home), make wonderful food to feed Krishna, for Krishna owns everything*. Besides, if one is in Krishna consciousness, one will succeed materially and spiritually without a doubt. Krishna is the Absolute Truth. Being in touch with the Supreme Truth, one will solve all one's problems effortlessly.

Lord Krishna is the Supreme Person (*"Isvarah paramah krsnah"*—*Brahma Samhita*). He is the Supreme Father (*"bija-pradah pita"*—BG 14.4). All living entities, humans, animals, plants and stones are His children. Everything is part and parcel of Krishna (*"mamaivamso jiva-loke jiva-bhutah sanatanah"*—BG 15.7). Krishna is the Supreme Whole and we are small parts. The parts' duty is to serve the whole as the limbs of the body serves the whole body.

Srila Prabhupada said that "Krishna consciousness is eternally a fact." It is hidden in our heart. One has to awaken it. One can do this by various methods of yoga as outlined in Chapter 4 of *The Bhagavad Gita*. In Satya Yuga the process was meditation, in Treta Yuga, it was *yajna* (sacrifice), in Dvarapa Yuga it was opulent worship. For this age, the best method is the chanting of the Holy Names given by Lord Chaitanya Mahaprabhu.

Sri Rupa Goswami outlined the stages of bhakti in his book, *Bhakti Rasamrita Sindhu*. In the beginning one should have just enough faith (*shraddha*) to take up the bhakti process. Then one should go to a temple, meet like-minded people, listen to talks on transcendental topics, eat *prasadam* and see *arati* (these are examples of *sadhu sanga*, or being in the association of spiritually minded people). When one enjoys the temple experience, one should start chanting the Holy Names, following the regulative principles (celibacy, eating vegetarian food, avoiding intoxicants and being truthful) and studying *The Bhagavad Gita* and other transcendental literature (*bhajana kriya*). One should gradually give up bad habits like intoxicants and *tamasic* food to attain *anartha nivritti*, freedom from life's obstacles. As one continues, one will have more faith, and will like to go to the temple often and chant regularly. One will be fixed in a new way of life (*nishta*) and be sure that one has found the truth. One will feel that one has found the right path. Faith will gradually grow into a deep conviction.

As one makes further progress, one comes to the stage of transcendental taste or *ruci*. Here the devotee enjoys the devotional process. Until this point, the devotional process is theoretical or abstract. With *ruci* one enjoys the beauty and truth of a Krishna conscious life. As one continues, one comes to divine attachment or addiction (*asakti*).

One cannot do without devotional service. One also does not like material pleasure or things. The next stage is divine emotion (*bhava*). One sometimes sheds tears, sometimes feels a pang of separation from Krishna. After *bhava* matures, one comes to the stage of divine love (*prema*). One gets absorbed and immersed in Krishna. One feels eternally related to Krishna and wishes to serve and please Krishna; one's love becomes permanent. Being on the bhakti path, one may sometimes dream of Krishna, Lord Chaitanya Mahaprabhu, Srila Prabhupada, Vrindavana and Mayapur, and devotees performing *sankirtan*. These dreams are signs of spiritual advancement. One should accept them as genuine. As the Holy Names and *The Bhagavad Gita* are the same as Krishna, so is a dream of Krishna. Once a devotee enjoys one's *sadhana*, one's perfection is guaranteed.

Krishna bhakti restores our consciousness back to its original pristine condition. One gradually realizes that one is not this body, mind or intelligence. One's essence is spirit soul or *atman*. One is a part and parcel of Krishna and thus one is His eternal servitor. One's pleasure lies in the service of Krishna. God is eternal, knowledgeable and blissful, and so are all the *jiva* souls.

Lord Sri Krishna Chaitanya Mahaprabhu said that Lord Krishna invested all potencies in His Holy Name. The chanting of His Holy Name brings immediate benediction. One feels relief and coolness from the heat of the material world. The Holy Names bring Vrindavana amongst us. One starts to see beauty all around oneself. The earth, water, sky, hills, trees, the living entities … everything takes on the beauty of Vrindavana. One also feels affection for every being and everything. This way Krishna, Vāsudeva, reveals Himself to His devotee. God is beauty, all attractive, and everything magnificent one sees. In Krishna consciousness one's existence becomes full of knowledge and joy. One becomes transcendentally happy and content.

Lord Krishna, God, is *sat cit ananda vigraha*. Because one is part and parcel of Krishna, one is also *sat cit ananda vigraha*, but in a minute portion. One is the same in quality but different in quantity with respect to Krishna, the Supreme Whole. For example, we are the same in chemical composition, but in minute quantity like an atom of water (H_2O) in the ocean. God has six opulences in full (*aisvarya viryasya sa yasha sriya jnana vairagya*), but one has them in minute quantities (*achintya-bheda-abheda tattva*). Also at the present moment, one's self or true nature is covered with material contamination. But by chanting the Holy Names and following *The Bhagavad Gita*, one can regain one's original nature. One can understand that one is part and parcel of Krishna, and one's real duty is to serve Him. One makes the transition from body consciousness to soul consciousness.

To serve Krishna is also a necessity for the soul because by serving Krishna one is in one's original position. For example, if a screw has fallen on the floor away from the machine, the screw is useless and the machine does not function properly, as the fallen soul is miserable away from Krishna. When the screw is placed back in the machine to serve it, the screw is in its rightful, original place and the machine functions properly. This pure understanding is Krishna consciousness. At this point, when one starts to serve Krishna, one's real life begins. When one serves Krishna, Krishna is pleased and the servitor also becomes happy and overcomes the three modes of material nature. One regains his or her original consciousness. An ordinary living entity chases after material happiness and is illusioned. She suffers pain, sorrow and anxiety. But a devotee, being in Krishna consciousness, enjoys unending bliss.

One is fortunate to be born human. With a human body comes higher intelligence. One should, therefore, live a better life than plants, insects and animals. In fact, one should seek the meaning of life; *athato Brahma jijnasa*—now is the time to enquire about Brahman. One should know who one really is, where one came from, where one is going, who is God, and how one can live a perfect human life. One inherently seeks knowledge (*jnana*), joy or happiness (*ananda*), and eternal healthy life (*sat*). As minute particles of God, *sat cit ananda*, it is natural for us to desire these things. Many great men and women (*mahajans*) before us also attained these things. All one needs to do is to follow these *mahajans*. Like them, one can also live a *mahajivan*, great life. One doesn't need to suffer like we do in lower forms of life. As humans, one can elevate oneself to a life of *sat cit ananda*. One must not waste time. As Prahlad Maharaja said, one must start Krishna consciousness from childhood (*"kaumāra ācaret prājño"*—SB 7.6.1). The sooner one starts the better, because one immediately sets out on a path of happiness and perfection.

Spiritual practice takes effort, but the result of penance is divine (*tapa divyam*). One purifies one's existence through *tapasya* and in the end one realizes our true nature. One becomes liberated from material existence; one becomes free from the three modes of material nature and the cycle of life, death, old age and disease, and becomes one's shining self. Without following *tapasya*, rules and regulations, one cannot attain our true nature. Without purifying our existence, one cannot understand God, because God or Krishna is pure (*pavitra*). One cannot enter fire without becoming fire, otherwise one will be burnt. One can know Krishna only when one becomes like Krishna in quality.

One should avoid sensory gratification, because then one gets more and more implicated in material life and one works towards another material body. Instead one should control one's senses by using them in the service of the Lord, become liberated and go home, back to Krishna. Live in the world but be not of it. Focus on Krishna. One's consciousness and activities should always be dovetailed with Krishna.

Ordinarily one is entangled in illusion or Maya. We think we are our bodies, nationality and status, which are impermanent. Because of this misconception, we are annoyed and unhappy. To get out of this unhappiness, one needs to take to Krishna consciousness. One needs to take the Holy Name of God and practice meditation on the deity form of God, Sri Radha Madhava, from the heart. To establish oneself in bhakti or devotion, one should live in the mode of goodness, or *sattva*. With bhakti yoga, one can transition from ego to essence. One should eat right, cultivate good habits, be devoted to Krishna, and avoid restlessness (*rajas*) and inertia (*tamas*). Ordinary people live in body consciousness and are in the modes of *rajas* and *tamas*. Their life is in constant flux and they suffer because of their forgetfulness of Krishna, like a prince who loses memory and lives in a slum.

One should acquire knowledge by studying science, philosophy, mathematics, literature and the *shastras*, which will help one to understand God. Lord Krishna explains the science of God in *The Bhagavad Gita*; that we are pure self or *atman*; and about our material world and the spiritual world, our relationship with God, karma and time.

Krishna consciousness is not difficult. Most of the time we think of food, shelter, entertainment, money and worldly affairs. Instead, one should focus on Krishna, His name, activities as detailed in *The Srimad Bhagavatam*, words as narrated in *The Bhagavad Gita*, pure devotees or *mahajans* and their lives as told in *The Chaitanya Charitamrita*. In this way one can always be in Krishna consciousness, or in Vrindavana. Instead of thinking of mundane things, one can switch to thoughts of Krishna. This will make our lives successful. Nothing is lost in taking to the *bhakti* path; giving up material pleasures for Krishna consciousness will not result in any lack of material comforts, as Krishna provides and cares for His devotees. We chant the

Lord's name, meditate on Him, and eat *prasadam*; as Prabhupada says, "what is the difficulty?" If we are sincere, it is easy to be in Krishna consciousness.

Thinking of Krishna, one will fulfill all material desires while attaining a higher consciousness. The result will be tremendous. One will have eternal life full of knowledge and bliss. One need just take the shelter of Krishna's lotus feet. No more anxiety or fear. *Ma sucah*. Everything will be taken care of. Just be, and be happy. We don't have to change our occupation or lifestyle. If a scientist, continue to be a scientist. If a farmer, continue farming. If a traveler, travel, especially to holy places. In Krishna consciousness, one will self-actualize, that is, become the best version of oneself. For example, if one is a teacher, one will be a very good teacher. If one is a doctor, one will be a very good doctor. All we have to do is chant Hare Krishna. This will guarantee success and perfection. We will be healthy, wealthy, wise and happy, for certain.

Mantra Meditation

In the Upanishads there is a beautiful story of two birds in a tree. Both birds have sparkling magnificent plumage. One bird sits on the top branch, calm and poised. The other one flits about from branch to branch, eats the fruits of the tree, some ripe and sweet, and some green and sour. Suddenly the bird understands that it does not have to do that, and it can be calm and poised like the first bird. It then flies off to the top branch. The first bird represents the Supersoul or Krishna within the heart, and the second bird represents the soul of the living entity.

Our pure self is actually serene and poised. But because it is covered with the three modes of material nature, it is restless. Our material self, or false self (ego), experiences the world, which is sometimes pleasant, sometimes unpleasant. When our material self finds its repose in Krishna consciousness, then we are happy. Ordinarily we find ourselves in a bewildered state in this world. We struggle to make sense of things. Fortunately, many *mahajans* before us faced similar situations and found answers. Rather than trying to reinvent things, we should follow in their footsteps. As *The Chaitanya Charitamrita* says (Madhya 17.86), "*Mahājano yena gataḥ sa panthāḥ*": follow in the footsteps of the *mahajans*. Following the path shown by the *mahajans*, we can make our life sublime and leave footprints in the sands of time.

The first thing we should do is find our true self. Who am I? Am I my body, my mind, my physical or mental acquisitions? These are all impermanent. Who am I, then? There is no doubt that I exist. That existence is my true essence. I am also conscious or aware. This conscious true existence is my soul, my actual self, or *atman* (*aham Brahmasmi*: I am Brahman and Lord Krishna is the Supreme Existence or Parabrahman).

I am but a small existence in this universe, a tiny, tiny part. The existences of all things and beings, including me, constitute the Cosmic Existence or God or Paramatma. As my soul permeates my body and my mind, the Universal Soul permeates the entire cosmos. Also, I am a person; so is God. So if God is not a person, how can I be a person, as everything is contained within God?

One should meditate on one's true self or pure existence and the Universal Self, because this is the path to know God and the actual reality. Our existence is like a small pond; God is like the big ocean. We are the same in quality but different in quantity. The soul is the same substance as the Supersoul, only a minute part of the Supersoul. The soul is a tiny part of the whole.

Our individual ego, which is composed of body, mind and intelligence, is impermanent. It begins with birth and ends with death. But our pure self is eternal. It doesn't take birth and it doesn't die. It is non-material. When we wake up in the morning, we are just conscious existence. In a few seconds, we identify ourselves with body, mind, learning, wealth, and other material conceptions.

Although our existence is a miniscule part of the Cosmic Existence, our relationship is very, very close to Krishna. It is like a drop of water related to the ocean. Both are the same in quality but different in quantity. Our souls are parts of the Cosmic Whole or God. The more we know about the self, God, the creation, and our connectedness, the better we live in Krishna consciousness. Our lives become enlightened.

God is realized in three successive phases, namely Brahman realization, Paramatma realization and Bhagavan realization (*"Brahmeti Paramatmeti Bhagavan iti sabdyate"*—SB 1.2.11). God, or Lord Krishna is *sat cit ananda vigraha*. God is the embodiment of eternal truth, knowledge and bliss. Living entities are indestructible, eternal Brahman (BG 8.3). To be Krishna conscious one must acquire the qualities of Krishna. To attain the Supreme Brahman, one must become Brahman first. When a devotee, by devotional service (chanting the Holy Names: *Hare Krishna, Hare Krishna, Krishna Krishna, Hare Hare, Hare Rama, Hare Rama, Rama Rama, Hare Hare*; eating *prasadam* and living in *sattva guna*), understands one is unborn, eternal and an imperishable soul, one comes to the understanding of God at the level of Brahman. At this stage a devotee knows *aham Brahmasmi*: I am spirit soul or pure existence. The devotee loses fear of death and becomes free of anxiety. A devotee is *"brahma-bhuta prasannatma na socati na kanksati"* and becomes joyful and free from material entanglements (BG 18.54).

By further meditation and devotional service, one understands not only the *sat* (truth) but also the *cit* (knowledge) aspect of Lord Krishna or God. At this stage the devotee clearly understands the world and other living entities, and understands that God is the Controller and the real Doer. The devotee is highly moral and ethical, and works in tune with God or the Universal Controller. The devotee gets direction from God within (*antaryami* or indweller), and cannot do anything harmful or unethical. The devotee may also develop mystic powers to perform miracles, like moving objects or manifesting things. Lord Krishna, being in everyone's heart, is the knower of everyone's activities.

Ananda realization is personal realization of God or Krishna. *Sat cit ananda*, all three aspects are understood; as Vyasadeva wrote in the Vedas, "*anandamaya abhyasat,*" Lord Krishna is eternally blissful. The devotee by worshipping Lord Sri Krishna, who is "*shyamasundara acintya-guna-svarupam,*" (beautiful as a rain cloud and the embodiment of infinite virtues, *Brahma Samhita* 5.38), understands that we are eternal loving servants of Him and attains Bhagavan realization (realization of God as a person). All living entities being born of Him, love Him. Lord Sri Krishna, as the Parent of the living entities, reciprocates love. At this stage, the devotee is full of love, bliss and knowledge. God is a person like us; God has His family, friends and associates in Goloka Vrindavana, as He did in earthly Vrindavana when He appeared there.

Brahman realization is the beginning of transcendental life. Paramatma and Brahman are contained in Bhagavan, the Supreme Person. Brahman is indestructible, eternal existence or *sat*, and manifests as Paramatma is cognition or knowledge (*cit*) plus eternal existence (*sat*). Bhagavan is *sat* plus *cit* plus *ananda* (bliss). All three states encompass *sat, cit* and *ananda*, but manifest with peace in the *sat* state, joy and knowledge in the *sat-cit* state, and full eternal knowledge and bliss in the third *sat-cit-ananda* state. All living entities exhibit these three *sat-cit-ananda* aspects in minute quantities. These qualities become fully manifest in the human form of life by developing bhakti yoga or Krishna consciousness.

The way to unite ourselves with the Cosmic Self is through meditation and worship. We are already one, but lack the realization thereof. To realize the truth, one can meditate on the deity form of Radha Krishna, do mantra meditation and worship God with flowers, incense and water, engaging our senses in the service of the Lord. The early morning, after a refreshing shower, is a good time for meditation. One should be clean and calm, because through meditation we are trying to connect with the Absolute Truth.

The eight step path of meditation is described in the *Yoga Sutra of Patanjali*. These eight steps are: *yama, niyama, asana, pranayama, pratyahara, dharana, dhyana* and *samadhi*. Yoga is a process of the sublimation of material energy into spiritual energy. Yoga means connecting our soul with the Supreme. Yoga removes the fluctuations of our mind: "*yogas citta vritti nirodha*" (Patanjali). Yoga is the control of senses for the purpose of concentration on Krishna.

The *sadhaka* must make a resolute determination (*sankalpa*) and commitment to achieve Krishna consciousness. Practice resolutely with sincerity and determination, and do not allow setbacks to stop continued spiritual efforts (*abhyas*). Have faith and conviction that the process will produce results (*shraddha*). Practice the remembrance of *vani* and the pastimes of Krishna and great devotees (*smriti*). *Prajna,* or prescience, develops in the *sadhaka*. For example, one can foresee the results of one's actions and can therefore make correct and beneficial decisions.

1. *Yama* consists of nonviolence (*ahimsa*), truthfulness (*satyam*), not stealing (*asteya*), celibacy (*brahmacharya*), and not accepting gifts (*aparigraha*).

Nonviolence means that one should remove cruelty from one's heart and be friendly to all living beings. Cruelty distorts one's consciousness and makes one ineligible to serve the Lord. Therefore one must not indulge in meat eating. When one becomes perfectly established in *ahimsa* all living entities also become friendly to one.

Truthfulness means speaking the truth without harming others and conducting oneself honestly. If one speaks and lives truthfully, one's thoughts, words and deeds become powerful. One's words and wishes will certainly manifest.

Asteya means a yogi shouldn't take another person's ideas and possessions. A person situated in *asteya* enjoys his own possessions and his words and wishes manifest.

When one is established in *brahmacharya* or celibacy, one's body and mind becomes strong and one's determination becomes unshakable. One becomes heroic, like Arjuna (also known as *Dhananjaya* or winner of wealth), and gets all the gifts of life. A *brahmachari* (male) or *brahmacharini* (female) is also one who practices the awareness of the Supreme Brahman by chanting the Holy Names and controlling the senses.

A person observing *aparigraha* automatically avoids karmic involvement, because gifts come with the karma of the givers. To avoid good and bad karma, giving and receiving must only be done in Krishna consciousness.

2.   *Niyama* consists of cleanliness of the body and mind (*saucha*), contentment in all circumstances (*santosha*), austerity (*tapas*), self-study (*svadhyaya*), and devotion to God or Krishna (*Isvar pranidhana*).

Saucha means one should take a bath and keep one's mind free from anger, jealousy, hate, greed and other negative emotions. Taking a bath cools one's body and mind and keeps one's devotion steady.

Santosha or contentment in all circumstances means one should be satisfied with one's own possessions and fortune. One should feel grateful to God for one's position in this world. This attitude helps one on the path of devotion.

Austerity (*tapas*) purifies oneself and increases the power of endurance and trains one's senses to be steady, allowing one to perform mantra meditation for long periods of time.

Self-study or introspection (*svadhyaya*) gives one clarity and insight about what one needs to do and understanding about oneself and Krishna. One's problems and bad habits come to light and one can understand how to improve oneself and one's interactions with the world. The study of the meaning of the words in scripture is a part of self-study, and leads to an understanding of the deeper meaning of the scriptures. Scrutinize and study the scriptures to understand their meaning and develop insight into bhakti yoga.

Isvar pranidhana or devotion to Krishna is achieved by daily mantra meditation (*japa*), worship of the deities, reading about Krishna, and meditating on Krishna to grow one's devotion and develop one's relationship with Krishna. All these steps lead one to joyfully and enthusiastically performing devotional service and becoming Krishna conscious.

3. *Asana* means steady comfortable posture. For meditation one should sit comfortably. The Buddha said, that one should sit as one strings a bow; the bow should be strung neither too tightly nor loosely. Hatha yoga postures are preparatory yoga for *asana* and meditation, but give untold benefits to body and health.

4.   *Pranayama* means control of the in and out breath, which steadies one's mind for meditation on Krishna and allows one to exist in the present moment.

5.   *Pratyahara* is recalling the senses inward to the spine, which follows *pranayama*. The sensory energy flows back to the heart or away from the senses and allows the mind to be focused or concentrated. Thoughts of eating or talking should be subdued.

6.   *Dharana* means concentration or focus on an object (light, deity) or spiritual quality (love, compassion) and culminates in concentration on the form of the Lord.

7.   *Dhyana* means steady concentration on Radha Krishna which follows from practice of *dharana*. The focused mind is directed toward the Holy Names and to the deity. One should stay in the state for half an hour or longer to chant 16 rounds of the Maha Mantra. One may feel bliss bubbling in the heart center. This is the sign of a successful meditation, and a devotee should attempt to preserve this state throughout the day.

8.   *Samadhi* means total absorption in Krishna's form and pastimes; one obtains total absorption of the mind in Krishna. At this stage one transcends one's material ego. There is only the soul (the devotee) and the Supersoul (Krishna).

Among all virtues, *brahmacharya* is foremost. It is the foundation of all other virtues. When one is established in *brahmacharya*, other virtues such as *ahimsa* and *satyam* start to blossom. One should practice spirituality from childhood centered in Krishna consciousness; then one's whole life becomes successful and happy. No one can be happy without following spiritual principles. The sooner one comes to spiritual life, the better it is. Otherwise, one will inevitably be entangled in material nature and the bodily concept of life, enduring hardships and sorrows. One will be further away from an actual blissful life.

The conscious animating principle is the soul, and the universal conscious animating principle is God. When the soul leaves the body, the body becomes lifeless. The soul is not physical; it is spiritual in nature. The soul cannot be detected, unlike energy or light, by instruments. But it certainly exists, because a lifeless body lacks only the soul, the animating principle.

In our daily lives we find many spiritual symptoms, which emanate from the pure self, such as love, affection, courage and flashes of insight. In dreams we experience our astral body (made of mind intelligence and ego), and one is in a different world which is complete in itself. Upon awakening, the astral world vanishes and one is in the material world once again. When in the astral world, it is real to the soul, and when in the material world, it is the current reality. When someone faints, one's consciousness becomes inactive. However, one's astral body may become activated and one may experience all sorts of things, such as light, peaceful presence of departed souls and even the Brahman aspect of God. Often these experiences in the astral world are transformative and retained after return to the material world.

According to the Taittiriya Upanishads, every one of us has five bodies. Each body is encased in (and subtler than) the previous body. The five bodies are:

1. *Ahnamaya kosha*, the material body built from food which can be cultivated with good food (*prasadam*) and exercise.

2. *Prahamaya kosha,* made up of the life force and cultivated with breath control or *pranayama*, sunshine and fresh air.

3. *Manamaya kosha,* composed of thought and cultivated with mantra meditation or *japa*.

4. *Vijananamaya kosha,* composed of intellect and cultivated by studying *shastra*.

5. *Anandamaya kosha,* composed of pure joy and cultivated through bhakti yoga.

When we wake up in the morning, for an instant we experience our true self; that life force with its non-reflective awareness (present moment awareness, without thought). Afterwards, our material world awareness floods into our consciousness. Sometimes in nature, we feel pure egoless awareness. We see trees, lakes, hills, all in harmony. Our consciousness is in the perfect present moment.

We can be in our pure state by consciously practicing *brahmacharya, ahimsa,* and truth. Every morning one should meditate on God (Krishna) and do *japa* by chanting the Hare Krishna Maha Mantra. One can synchronize one's chanting with one's breath while visualizing the deities or Krishna. Breath control or *pranayama* and the flow of breath and mind through the chakras assist in controlling the mind during meditation. After some time, the chanting and breath will become automatic (*ajapa*). This process anchors one's mind to the Holy Names and the deity form. One can tell that one's meditation is successful when one feels joy.

To meditate, one should sit on a soft cushion with one's back straight but unstrained (*asana*). It is good to take a shower prior to meditation to feel fresh and energetic (*saucha*). One should put the left leg on the right leg. This is a half lotus posture. Sitting in this way will eventually allow a yogi to sit in full lotus posture. Then one should put one's right palm on the left palm and lightly press the palm against the legs and abdomen.

The spiritual aspirant or *sadhaka* then takes a long breath and breathes out gently. One should repeat this four more times. Now, one should visualize gurus and deities. One should do *pranayama*. Take a breath through the left nostril while closing the right nostril with the right hand thumb to the count of 10. Then, one should hold the breath for the count of 10. One should release the breath to the count of 10 through the right nostril while closing the left nostril with one's right hand index finger. Repeat the process in reverse order, that is, first breath through the right nostril, hold and breathe out through the left nostril. One may do this *pranayama* routine 10 times in one sitting. *Pranayama* allows *prana* or life force to travel up and down through the various chakras of the spine. The chakra at the bottom of the spine is called Muladhara; four inches above it is Svadhisthana. The back of the navel is the Manipura chakra. Close to the heart is Anahata. At the neck is the Visuddha chakra. In the center of our forehead is the Ajna chakra. Three inches above the crown of the head (*brahma randhra*), starting at the crown, is the Sahasrara chakra. These chakras can be felt by yoga practitioners. For example, one feels love or compassion at the heart or Anahata center. We feel a vortex in the forehead or Ajna chakra when thinking deeply.

By *pranayama*, one takes the life force or Kundalini by the incoming breath from the bottom of the spine, through all the chakras, to the Ajna chakra as a silver stream of light. Then, one brings it down again through all the chakras in reverse order, to the Muladhara chakra by the outgoing breath. During *pranayama*, one's mental attention follows the breath as it travels through the chakras. In *samadhi*, the Sahasrara chakra lights up.

When the Muladhara chakra (at the base of the spine) is awakened, one's fear disappears. A person becomes anchored in the earth element and becomes very grounded. This is the beginning of true human qualities and life. Before this chakra is awakened, the person exists by eating, sleeping, mating and defending.

When the Svadhisthana chakra (four inches above the base of the spine) becomes awakened, one becomes materially detached and satisfied. This is the water center. The person becomes creative, as lust, anger and greed diminish.

When the Manipura chakra (back of the navel) becomes awakened, the person becomes energetic, healthy, has high self-esteem, humility and confidence in oneself, undisturbed by other people's opinions. One becomes prosperous and lives in Manipura, the city of jewels. Digestion and overall health improves. One sees beauty in the world around one, and may develop psychic powers to heal oneself and others. This is the fire center. When these first three chakras are awakened, the person lives a moral, thoughtful, healthy life and has worldly success. These three lower chakras result in the living of a very good life.

When the Anahata chakra (heart) is awakened, the person feels compassion for all living entities. This is a very important chakra, the air center, as it is the beginning of spiritual progress. Pure emotions arise at this center, such as gratitude, love, affection, kindness, generosity and pure unselfish desires. One becomes poetic, and feels connected to the universe.

When the Visuddha chakra (neck) is awakened, the person becomes purified and is free of material contamination. One's thoughts are coherent. At this stage, a person's prayer or mantra becomes effective. One's speech is convincing and one's voice is appealing. One's speech manifests. This is the center of space.

When the Ajna chakra (forehead) is awakened, the person becomes intuitive and self-controlled. The center is also the third eye. This is the center of the mind. One's mind's commands are obeyed by the senses. The person knows the minds of others. This is also the center of vision and wisdom. At this stage there is only *atman* and Paramatma (the devotee and Krishna); the person is beyond the material world.

When the Sahasrara chakra (three inches above the crown of the head) is awakened, the person goes into *Samadhi*. He or she is able to know God and function transcendentally. One is full of knowledge and bliss. One is Krishna conscious. This stage is transformative. As Swami Vivekananda said, "When a man goes into *samadhi*, if he goes into it a fool, he comes out a sage." The Sahasrara chakra is full of splendour and awakens one to infinite knowledge and intelligence. The Sahasrara chakra was awakened for Arjuna in his cosmic vision where a thousand suns rose at once in the sky.

Our cosmos or Brahmanda (cosmic egg) with its planets, stars, moons and comets is an ordered, harmonious whole. The cosmos is the embodiment of Krishna, where all living entities exist. Vāsudeva is the objective reality. Everything magnificent is a manifestation of Lord Krishna. Even if something is destroyed, something new comes in its place and no chain reaction of destruction takes place; it is as if a leaf or flower falls from a tree, but a new bud is formed. The tree remains; our cosmos remains. The galaxies, stars, planets and all are in cosmic harmony and are bound by cosmic law. It is, therefore, also our duty to live in harmony with the cosmic laws. We must live in harmony with fellow beings, animals, trees, rivers, mountains, planets, moons and all. This is the eternal religion or Sanatana Dharma. The twin pillars of *dharma* are *satyam* or truth and *ahimsa* or nonviolence.

As our pure consciousness (self) animates the entire body, so does the Cosmic Self animate the entire universe. Because we are persons with will, emotion, reason and individuality, therefore the Cosmic Self is also a person.

Everything that exists in the universe is eternal. Whatever exists cannot be nonexistent; only the form may be changed (BG 2.16). We know by physics that energy cannot be created or destroyed. The same is true for our pure consciousness or soul. The soul is spiritual energy. Our souls are, in truth, never born and never die. Our physical births or deaths are simply Illusions. The soul migrates through many bodies and many apparent births and deaths until it attains *moksha* or liberation. This cycle of birth and death is called reincarnation or *punarjanma*.

The quality of life we live depends on our actions or karma. Our past actions determine our present and our future will be shaped by our current actions; this is the law of karma. In the material world, this is Newton's third law (every action has an equal and opposite reaction). Laws of the physical world have a spiritual equivalent. If we live our life according to spiritual principles, we are rewarded and live happy lives. If we do not follow the spiritual laws, we inevitably suffer, as it is a law.

As soon as one starts on the spiritual path, one's karma starts to weaken and dissipate. Everything in one's life starts to improve. When one attains self-realization or enlightenment, one becomes free from karma and material life. For the remaining part of one's life one does not produce any karma. Also, one won't reincarnate because one has no karma to work out. One *can* reincarnate however, if one wishes, to help others spiritually. On the other hand, ordinary living entities continue to go through repeated birth and death by no choice of their own until they attain spiritual perfection.

Our human life provides us with a great opportunity for spiritual advancement. Human life is very rare; one attains human life after many reincarnations as plants, animals and insects. Human life is meant for spiritual enlightenment, because only in human life is it possible for a *jiva* to practice bhakti yoga or Krishna consciousness. One can attain perfection of life simply by living a life in the mode of pure goodness, following *brahmacharya* principles, chanting the Holy Names and meditation. If our daily life is immersed in the thought of Krishna, progress and eventual enlightenment are certain.

The Sri Chaitanya Charitamrita states that our pure self was originally with God but because we wished to experience the material world, we came here. We forgot our actual nature when we took material bodies. We became subject to the laws of the material world, we started to accumulate karma, and all our troubles began. Our happiness and freedom were lost to this world governed by the three modes of material nature: *sattva*, *raja*, and *tama*. *Sattva* is purity, *raja* is passion, and *tama* is dull foolishness. A *sattvic* person's head is clear and alert. He introspects; he searches for a way to be happy. In *sattva guna*, one restarts spiritual life. When one becomes a devotee, one transcends all *guna*s or modes and once again becomes situated in the spiritual world, which is beyond all *gunas*. Unfortunately, with the start of our spiritual journey, our troubles do not immediately end. The *sadhaka* should live a life of purity in *sattva guna*. One should shower or bathe every day, wear clean clothes, and eat *sattvic* food, such as fruits, vegetables, and milk. One should study scriptures and keep one's mind on Krishna. This will keep one's *prana* or life force pure. One becomes wise simply by pure living. One develops intelligence and discrimination for every situation in life.

The material world is based on the bodily concept of life. However, our soul is spiritual. So, the more one gives in to one's bodily demands or sense pleasures, the more one becomes distant from one's actual spiritual nature. That is why one needs to restrict one's senses. One should use discrimination as to one's needs and wants. One needs to keep oneself healthy and fit, and avoid indulgence in the senses. Do activities that are favourable for spiritual development or Krishna consciousness, and abstain from activities that are unfavourable for spiritual development.

Because we live in the material world, we need to know about matter, plants, animals and society. Knowledge is indeed power. However, it is more important is to know oneself. Self-knowledge by studying *The Srimad Bhagavad Gita* gives insight into personal strengths and makes one steady, without which, one is erratic and dull like an intoxicated person. Without self-knowledge, we cannot be happy; parents should teach children about spirituality early. Knowing about the soul, God, truth and nonviolence will certainly make children successful. Children should be encouraged to engage in professions suitable to their dominant *guna* and disposition. This will ensure both material and spiritual success. They should be told that they are to do good things for themselves and others.

The consciousness of human beings is at a much higher level than the consciousness of animals like dogs, horses and cows, and the consciousness of these animals is also at a higher level than squirrels, rabbits or fish. Human consciousness has reason, imagination, emotion and will. However, human beings can attain an even higher consciousness called "super consciousness" through meditation. This breakthrough has been made by a great number of people. It is our duty to advance our consciousness. Otherwise, we remain at a slightly higher level than horses and dogs, and our lives become mundane. Being born as a human determines the ordinary life we live, but by choosing a life of pure living, study and meditation, we can raise our consciousness to a higher level.

Only in our super conscious state can we realize the meaning of our lives. Plants and animals live in simple consciousness. Most of humanity lives in ordinary consciousness, barely aware of true happiness. Sometimes content, sometimes delighted, these feelings are short lived, and most of humanity quickly reverts back to anxiety and unhappiness. For most people, enlightenment is a remote possibility, but the lives of many great people show that one can attain this state of super consciousness by steady spiritual practice, if one just chooses to start. Many great people, unknown to the world, have achieved enlightenment. Anyone can become enlightened. True happiness comes from awakening to one's true self. This happiness is permanent. Waves of joy wash up on the shore of one's being.

An enlightened person feels connectedness to all living entities and the entire creation, and one feels empathy for all living entities and the pain and happiness of others. One can see the world with great clarity, can understand the motives and thoughts of others, and has an understanding of the physical world. One feels great love for Krishna and Krishna's creation. One lives in unending bliss.

As Swami Sri Yukteswar said, when one starts on the spiritual path, all things improve. One becomes healthy, wealthy and wise. When one advances further, one comes to know one's relationship with Krishna, the world and fellow beings. Gradually one becomes more and more blissful, and that is soul living.

The Brihadaranyak Upanishad tells us a story about happiness. The heavenly gods became bored of their opulence, food, drink and music, as all was readily available. Humans grew food working hard in their fields; they became very angry when birds ate their crops. The demons enjoyed scaring and tormenting other people, and they became tired of it. Then the heavenly gods, humans and demons went to Brahma and told him about their unhappiness. Brahma listened carefully, said the single syllable "da," and vanished.

The gods, humans and demons were perplexed and pondered about what happened. The heavenly gods thought "da" meant *dama* or self-restraint. They stopped indulgences and became happy. The humans thought "da" meant *dana* or charity. They gave food to the birds and became happy. The demons thought "da" meant *daya* or compassion. They stopped persecution and became happy.

Ordinary people are actually a mix of godly, human and demonic tendencies. We should all therefore practice these virtues (self-restraint, charity and compassion) as well as meditation on Krishna. That will lead us to true happiness. Without devotion to God, the practice of virtue alone does not lead to bliss.

Through pure life, *brahmacharya*, and chanting the Holy Names, the impossible becomes possible. One must realize that one is spirit or soul, not one's ego, which is body, mind, and intelligence. When one is aware of one's actual self and lives a Krishna conscious life, one's life becomes amazing. One becomes a devotee and has a deeper understanding and awareness of everything. One is healthy and energetic. One's meditation is deep and one steadily progresses towards illumination and bliss.

Originally we were with God in Goloka Vrindavana. Our consciousness was pure and pristine. When we descended into the material world our trouble started, and that pure consciousness was lost. It is extremely difficult to return to the original state on our own. We need God's blessing; we need guru *kripa* (mercy of Krishna's representatives, such as Prabhupada, Bhaktisiddhanta Thakur, Sri Narottama Das Thakur), and also instructions or *vani* from other *mahajans*.

Chanting of the Holy Names changes our material consciousness into spiritual consciousness; gradually we return to our pure state again and come to know our relationship with God. Our pure self is a part of the Cosmic Self, which is the Whole. We are like little ponds; God is like the mighty ocean. A small part of a cauliflower is just like a whole cauliflower. As in a fractal, we are part of the whole universe. The same cosmic laws operate through us, so it is our duty to be in harmony with the cosmos. We feel happy when we realize that our *atman* is a part of the Brahman, as children feel happy and proud of their parents.

Royal Knowledge

In Chapter 4 of *The Bhagavad Gita*, Lord Krishna said to Arjuna that He is giving him Brahma vidya, which is mysterious in nature. He also said that He gave this knowledge earlier to the Sun god Vivasvan and Vivasvan gave this to his son Manu and so on. Although this knowledge is eternal, it was lost in the course of time. In Chapter 9, Lord Krishna calls this knowledge *"raja vidya, raja guhya"* (royal science, royal secret). What is this transcendental knowledge which is so valuable, confidential and mysterious in nature? This is the crest jewel of all knowledge, like a touchstone that transforms a fool into a sage. By knowing this knowledge, everything else is known. This knowledge of Krishna consciousness was given to Arjuna by Krishna on the battlefield of Kurukeshetra in *The Bhagavad Gita*: We are not our bodies but spirit soul. We are part and parcel of the Supreme Whole, Krishna, and our duty is to serve Him, heart and soul. We are to dovetail our consciousness to Krishna consciousness. We are naturally inclined to serve Krishna like a child wants to serve his or her mother. A child is born of the mother, so a child spontaneously loves the mother; as Lord Krishna is our Supreme Parent, we cannot but love Him.

As previously mentioned, Lord Chaitanya Mahaprabhu said that *"jīvera 'svarūpa' haya—kṛṣṇera 'nitya-dāsa,'"* the constitutional position of all living entities is to serve Krishna (CC Madhya 20.108). However, only in the human form of life can we understand this position, because with the human body comes superior intelligence; animals, insects, birds and plants don't have that. In the human form of life we start to question our existence and the world. We wish to know what life is about, where we came from, where we are going, why we suffer, is there a God (a central authority), what does He look like and so on. The Vedanta-sutra says *"athato Brahma jijnasa."* Now that you have got a human form of life, it is time to enquire about Brahman.

The first lesson of *The Srimad Bhagavad Gita* is that we are not our bodies but eternal, unborn souls inside our material bodies (*dehi*). We must therefore act in spiritual consciousness and not in bodily consciousness.

Sage Rsabhadeva said to his sons that our human lives are not to be wasted on sense gratification, but to attain Krishna consciousness, which we have missed in countless lives. A life of eating, sleeping, mating and defending (*ahara, nidra, bhaya* and *maithuna*) is for animals. The special prerogative of a human life is that we can question the meaning of life or enquire about Brahman.

Our real life is a Krishna conscious life. We are made in the image of God, as a child takes after their parents. *"Mamaivamso jiva-loke jiva-bhutah sanatanah"*: all living entities are but sparks of Krishna (BG 15.7). We exist on account of Krishna; therefore, we live our real life when we become a devotee of Krishna.

The universe is governed by Santana Dharma or the eternal principle of righteousness. The entire creation is upheld by *dharma*. *Dharma*, or cosmic law, is also an intrinsic quality of all living or material entities. For the sun, moon and stars it is harmonious motion in space. For living entities, it is to serve God or Krishna. When we repose our love and activities in Krishna we are happy. Our *dharma* is to serve Krishna; that's our intrinsic duty or property. Water's property is to wet. Fire's property is to light up or burn. Our soul's property is to be in tune with Krishna. When the universal *dharma* or individual *dharmas* are not aligned with the Lord, Sri Krishna descends to rectify the situation.

After many, many lives the living entities grow wise and surrender to Krishna. One understands that God is real, great and infinite, and one is minute or infinitesimal. It is one's duty to serve the infinite God and make one's life successful.

Krishna is our Supreme Friend and well-wisher ("*suhrdam sarva-bhutanam*"—BG 5.29). We are His fragmental parts. Our happiness is in being with Him. He is our Father-Mother, the Original Parent. We are divine children. We are happy only when we are with our Divine Parent.

The lives of ordinary people are mostly covered with *raja guna* (passion) and *tama guna* (ignorance). Seldom are they in *sattva guna* (goodness). They live ordinary dull lives, eating, sleeping, mating and defending. They seek sensory happiness, mainly of the belly. Those people in *raja* and *tama guna* don't question the meaning of life. After many lives those people in *sattva guna*, if they are fortunate, question the meaning of life. Why are we born? Where are we going? What is the aim of life? What happens to us after death? Is there a God?

By the mercy of Sri Chaitanya Mahaprabhu, who is Krishna Himself, we know that the meaning of life is to become a devotee of Krishna or God. When we are in our constitutional position (*nitya Krishna dasa*), when we know the science of God (Krishna tattva), our life becomes meaningful, truly glorious. We become eternal, all-knowing and full of infinite bliss. Without Krishna consciousness, without Krishna *tattva*, our lives are hollow and empty, without any significance.

It is only natural for us to serve Krishna. Krishna is our *mata, dhata, pitamaha*. We come from Krishna. We are eternally and intimately related to Krishna, with a bond that can never be broken. Before coming to the material world, we were in blissful service of the Lord. In the material world, we should continue to do so. If we don't, we will get ensnared by Maya and make mistakes after mistakes. We live a bewildered existence and suffer. We think that the pursuit of material knowledge and wealth will make us happy. But the material world is steeped in Maya, the play of the three modes of material nature, rooted in ignorance. Ignorance or darkness cannot give us an enlightened life. Our hopes and activities will be baffled (*"moghasa mogha-karmano"*—BG 9.12). We do not wish to live in darkness. Our soul craves light: *"asato ma sat gamaya"*—Pavamana Mantra, Brhadaranyaka Upanishad. We wish for knowledge. *Prajnanam Brahma*.

We are not the body. We are not our mind, intelligence or ego. We are spirit souls. The soul hankers after the Supersoul or Krishna. Our real life is not in material acquisition or in material knowledge or sense pleasure, but in Krishna consciousness. Our soul's true activity is bhakti or Krishna consciousness. As in Paramahansa Yogananda's poem, *God, God, God*:

In waking, eating, working, dreaming, sleeping,

Serving, meditating, chanting, divinely loving

My soul will constantly hum, unheard by any,

God! God! God!

This is our soul's function, and therein lies our actual happiness.

Lord Sri Krishna Chaitanya Mahaprabhu taught that in Kali Yuga, Lord Krishna has incarnated as the Holy Names: *Hare Krishna, Hare Krishna, Krishna Krishna, Hare Hare, Hare Rama, Hare Rama, Rama Rama, Hare Hare*. This sound has all the potencies of Lord Krishna. In fact, the Holy Name is even more powerful than Krishna. The Holy Name of Krishna can rescue anybody and everybody. The Holy Name and Krishna are non-different.

By chanting the Maha Mantra, our hearts get cleansed and we become purified and established in *shuddha sattva* (pure goodness). We become capable of understanding spiritual truths and Krishna consciousness. Our actual life is beyond the modes of material nature. When ignorance is removed, when restlessness is removed, then our soul is awakened and our real life begins. Our real life is Krishna consciousness, which is rooted in the soul. In Krishna bhakti, our body, mind, senses, intelligence are all absorbed in the service of the Lord. Chanting the Holy Name brings us to that stage. The Holy Name is a *cintamani* (touchstone), the crest jewel that brings our soul to the spiritual world.

Our real business is to lovingly serve the Lord, Lord Sri Krishna. Krishna is God (*"isvarah paramah krsnah sac-cid-ananda-vigrahah"—Brahma Samhita*) because He has six major opulences (wealth, strength, fame, beauty, knowledge and renunciation) and a myriad of other opulences. Lord Krishna also showed to Arjuna His Universal Form containing everything within Himself. He appears *yuga* to *yuga* in His transcendental forms. Therefore, Krishna is God and the only God. We don't need proof that Krishna is God, just as we do not need proof that the sun or the earth exist. Krishna is the Supreme Whole and we are part and parcel of Krishna. A part's duty is to serve the whole, as a finger's duty is to serve the whole body. Similarly our duty is to serve God. This is our real occupation and it brings us to our normal condition (willingly and lovingly devoted to serve in happiness).

By serving the Lord our lives become pleasurable, as a mother becomes happy by feeding the child. In the same way, when we lovingly serve Krishna, who is our dearmost Person, we are happy. When Krishna is pleased, there is an incessant flow of joy and knowledge in us from Him. We become aware of our eternal identity as a soul and our lives become perfect. The more and more we become spiritualized, the more we become impervious to material suffering. When we serve Krishna, our material and subtle bodies both become spiritualized.

We should abide in our true nature and live in the glory of God. At the present moment our conception of the self is totally wrong. We think we are our bodies, ethnicities, nationalities, profession, wealth and knowledge, but we are not these designations. These conceptions are the false ego and impermanent. Our true self is covered by Maya or the three modes of material nature. Like a person in delirium or intoxicated, one is not one's normal self. When a person knows one's actual self and abides in Krishna consciousness in loving surrender to Krishna, when one is no longer in delusion, then one is a devotee, a *mahatma* in one's normal condition (truly sane).

By chanting the Hare Krishna Maha Mantra, one becomes gradually enlightened and engages in eternal all-knowing and blissful service of the Lord. This is the platform of perpetual happiness and our ultimate goal of existence.

Living beings, prior to coming to the material world, made a promise to serve Krishna (*"bhajibo boliyā ese saṁsāra-bhitare"*—*Jiv Jago Jiv Jago*, by Bhaktivinoda Thakura). However, after coming to the material world, they forgot the promise due to ignorance and became entangled in the web of material nature. Lord Chaitanya Mahaprabhu, the most munificent incarnation of Krishna, gave us medicine for curing our delusion. He gave us the Holy Names to reawaken our memory and re-engage us in the loving service of the Lord.

The Vedas talk about the three modes of material nature that govern our lives. Being in *sattva guna*, one acquires knowledge (*jnana*). In *raja guna*, one becomes too active which leads to misery. In *tama guna*, one is in darkness and delusion. By clean, plain living and high thinking (like introspection, or studying science and philosophy) one can be in *sattva guna*. Although in this mode (goodness and *jnana*) life is somewhat pleasurable, it does not free us from *janma, mrityu, jara* and *vyadhi* (birth, death, old age and disease) and does not give us the understanding of the meaning of life (i.e. significance and purpose of existence). In *raja guna* and *tama guna* our life is simply suffering and ignorance interspersed with some sensory pleasures.

One can, however, transcend all these modes by becoming a devotee of the Lord (BG 7.14). When one understands that it is only natural to be a devotee of Krishna (like a child devoted to her mother) and one engages in the processes of bhakti yoga (*srvanam, kirtanam, Vishnu smaranam, pada sevanam, arcanam, vandanam, dasyam, sakhyam, atma nivedanam*), one transcends the three modes and lives a natural blissful life.

To be successful in our devotional life we should control our senses and mind. The senses are strong and impetuous. They don't allow us to focus our mind on Krishna. The easiest way to control the senses is by engaging them in the service of the Lord. For example, if we offer nice food to Krishna and then eat the *prasadam*, we control our tongue. Similarly, if we offer flowers and incense to Lord Krishna, then by smelling the flowers and incense, we purify our sense of smell. By hearing Krishna katha, we purify our sense of hearing as well as our hearts, like Maharaja Ambarisa and Maharaja Parikshit. Thus, by devotional service, we can control all our senses and the urges of the body. We become steady.

To control the mind one should meditate on the beautiful form of Shyamasundara Krishna, with a flute in His hand, His beautiful face decorated with peacock feathers and His eyes blooming like lotus flowers. Then, we can focus and concentrate our mind at the lotus feet of our Lord Sri Krishna. We, along with all other living entities such as animals and plants, are not our bodies but spiritual sparks of the Supreme Spirit, from whom everything emanates. Only with this understanding can we see Krishna as Bhagavan.

If we are spiritual beings, we should also act spiritually. Realizing that we are spirits and part and parcels of Krishna grants us pure happiness, which is Krishna consciousness. It is natural for us to depend on Krishna as a little child depends on her mother. By the devotional process of hearing and chanting, we dovetail our consciousness with the Supreme consciousness and we become a surrendered soul. We do whatever Krishna wishes us to do. Being connected to God we function constitutionally, and our lives become meaningful and blessed.

By chanting the Holy Names we cleanse our heart of doubts, misgivings and ignorance. If we study *The*

Bhagavad Gita, The Srimad Bhagavatam and *The Sri Chaitanya Charitamrita* in that purified state, Lord Krishna's words and activities resonate in our hearts. We begin to realize the Lord's *lila* and become enlightened. Understanding God is the same as seeing Him because Krishna is Absolute.

When we attain transcendental knowledge, that is, knowledge of Krishna and our relationship with Him, we will never be deluded. We will have an eternal life of knowledge and bliss in devotion to Krishna. He is our Original Parent, our ultimate *dham* (abode) of contentment. Knowing which, one never falls into delusion (*"yaj jnatva punar moham"* —BG 4.35).

Knowledge is of the utmost importance for a Krishna conscious life. Knowledge is light; knowledge is power. Without knowledge we are in darkness. Even our ordinary life of prescribed duties becomes difficult without knowledge. Children should be taught spiritual knowledge along with science, arts and philosophy. Children should be taught that as living entities, they are a part of the universe, the Cosmic Whole, and need to live in harmony with the cosmos to have any happiness. They should be given spiritual engagements like chanting, reading books about devotees and helping in the *arati* by collecting flowers, making garlands and preparing the sandalwood paste. Children should be obedient and live a *brahmachari* life, because without this one will not progress. For students, learning is *tapasya* (austerity). They should be focused on acquiring knowledge and building character. Sri Rama showed obedience to His father by going into exile, which was unfair, but resulted in Rama destroying Ravana and establishing *dharma* and peace on earth. Lakshmana gained enormous power by observing *brahmacharya*, and was able to vanquish Ravana's son, Indrajit. Princess Savitri lived a pure and chaste life and gained such spiritual power that she was able to convince Yamaraja, the lord of death, to give life back to her deceased husband.

In *The Bhagavad Gita*, knowledge is compared to a raft (*plava*) that can cross over the ocean of nescience (BG 4.36). When we are born, we are in total darkness and delusion. We need knowledge, both spiritual and material, as well as the guidance of parents and *acaryas*. We should not only acquire spiritual knowledge and neglect material knowledge. Material knowledge is needed for a healthy and prosperous life, and to serve Krishna nicely. Material knowledge also helps us to better understand spiritual laws. For example, we can understand the law of karma by Newton's third law and we can understand indestructibility of the soul by knowing of the indestructibility of energy. So *jnana* is essential for advancement of life. Additionally, *jnana* burns up karma and purifies us. By the boat of knowledge we can safely and fearlessly come to the lotus feet of the Lord. One also becomes intelligent by learning. Lord Krishna does not reveal Himself to the foolish and unintelligent (BG 7.25).

Spiritual knowledge begins with the enquiry "who am I?" In *The Bhagavad Gita*, Lord Krishna says that we are not the body but soul or spirit and part and parcel of Him, and we should surrender to Him in bhakti (BG 15.7 and 18.66). The soul is called *dehi* (an occupant of the body) and when the soul leaves the body, the body is useless. If we are not the body, but spirit, then what is the function of the spirit? The function of the spirit soul is Krishna consciousness or to be reinstated in our constitutional position as an eternal servitor of Lord Sri Krishna. That is our duty and our only duty.

Bhakti Yoga

Lord Sri Krishna said a yogi (meditator) is better than a *karmi* or *jnani*, and among the yogis, the topmost is a *bhakta* (practitioner of bhakti yoga). Through karma yoga and jnana yoga, one can realize God as Brahman, which is the impersonal aspect of God. As a *bhakta*, one establishes a personal relationship with Parabrahman or Lord Sri Krishna. A devotee loves Lord Sri Krishna in a personal relationship, as a parent, friend, servant or beloved. This is the highest stage of God realization.

If one engages in devotional service, one may think, what about worldly duties? One should perform both devotional service and worldly duties in Krishna consciousness. No one starves by becoming Krishna conscious. God will take care of everything. By serving Krishna, a devotee becomes Krishnized; as an iron rod in contact with fire takes on the quality of fire, Krishna's devotee takes on the qualities of Krishna, and thus Lord Krishna's opulences flow into the life of the devotee. The devotee becomes healthy, wealthy, knowledgeable, kind, compassionate, insightful and takes on many other good qualities. In Krishna consciousness, we are in our original condition; all things come to us automatically.

There is nothing as purifying and sublime as spiritual knowledge. By Krishna's mercy, if we can deeply understand that we are spirit souls, part and parcel of the Supersoul and our natural duty is to serve the Supersoul or Krishna, our lives become perfect at once. By worshipping Krishna we establish ourselves in the

Supreme Self. Although the Krishna conscious devotee continues to live in the material world, because of his understanding, the devotee lives in Goloka Vrindavana. The knowledge of Krishna and our relationship with Him acts like a mighty ship that cannot be buffeted by the waves and winds of the material world. A devotee is safe and serene by the mercy of the Lord.

Happily do worldly duties like cooking, cleaning, farming, building, teaching, healing and so on, for the satisfaction of Vishnu (Krishna). By doing these works, one participates in the maintenance of the world. Because one acts being aware of Krishna, one does not accrue any karma, good or bad, but only progresses in Krishna consciousness *("yajnarthat karmano 'nyatra loko 'yam karma-bandhanah"* —BG 3.9). All worldly activities become spiritualized. Work done as a sacrifice for Vishnu must be performed. In this way one can always remain in divine consciousness and will be materially and spiritually opulent. One will be nicely engaged with the world at large, but won't be involved in it. Actually, one will be living the Vrindavana life.

Lord Sri Krishna says *"yoga-sthah kuru karmani"*: do your activity by linking yourself to Me, the Supreme consciousness. One may be studying for an exam, working in a job or enjoying the scenery by a beach, but one is never separated from Him because one is always immersed in Him (in Krishna consciousness). Physically, one is in the material world, but by dint of Krishna consciousness one is in the spiritual realm.

By bhakti yoga, one links oneself with the Supreme. When one chants the Holy Names, one is in touch with

Krishna and is no longer on the bodily platform; one is spirit, part and parcel of Krishna. Peace, love, happiness, joy, knowledge, everything flows into us automatically. As spirit one becomes absorbed in devotion to the Supreme Spirit. The after effect of chanting or devotional service continues throughout the day. One may be doing other things, but one is still in Krishna consciousness. One's mind remains calm (*shama*) like a deep blue lake undisturbed by the wind. Peacefulness is the very basis (*urgrund*, or fundamental ground state) of brahminical qualities like *dama*, *tapa*, *saucha*, *jnana* and *vijnana*. The peaceful mind of a Krishna conscious person is an ocean of good qualities.

All humans seek peace and happiness (wellbeing, contentment and joy) and success (health, wealth and wisdom). To enjoy happiness, one needs to develop one's intelligence or consciousness. Without proper intelligence one cannot perceive peace, happiness, beauty and other subtleties. At this moment one's consciousness is filled with worry, anxiety and fear. One's mind is hazy. One needs to cleanse one's mind. One needs to wake up. One's vision should be clear; one's perceptions should be sharp. These things can be attained by practicing Krishna consciousness.

In His infinite mercy, Lord Sri Krishna Chaitanya Mahaprabhu said in *Shikshashtakam*, "Let there be all victory for the chanting of the Holy Name of Lord Krishna, which can cleanse the mirror of the heart and stop the miseries of the blazing fire of material existence." By chanting the Holy Names, one receives the mercy of the Lord. The devotees' consciousness is purified and Lord Krishna awards transcendental intelligence ("*dadami buddhi-yogam tam*"—BG 10.10).

Krishna consciousness is the platform of happiness. When one chants the Holy Names, listens to Krishna katha or just meditates on Krishna's form, one's body feels wellbeing, one's mind becomes tranquil, one beholds beauty in the sky, nature, people, animals, insects—in everything. *Vāsudeva sarvam iti*, everything is Krishna. One feels the cooling touch of the breeze. One feels the golden warmth of the setting sun. In an orb of happiness, one reposes oneself at the lotus feet of the Lord like a honey bee.

One is spirit and one is subordinate to the Supreme Spirit. When one works from this conviction, then one is in Krishna consciousness and one is truly happy (*"sukhena brahma-samsparsam"*—BG 6.28). By mantra yoga, the chanting of the Holy Names, one cleanses one's mind and enters into a meditative union with the Supreme Spirit. One feels a bubble of joy envelope oneself. One feels a knowingness of everything. One feels one is forever, one feels safe (*sat cit ananda*). When one carries these feelings within oneself throughout the day and night, one is in complete Krishna consciousness. Ever new joy is God. Ever new knowledge (insight) is God. Knowing that one lives forever as Krishna's servitor, is God. In waking, eating, working, dreaming, sleeping, one always invokes the joy of God.

Rise up early in the morning, refreshen yourself, take a shower, eat some *prasadam* and then chant the Holy Names: *Hare Krishna, Hare Krishna, Krishna Krishna, Hare Hare, Hare Rama, Hare Rama, Rama Rama, Hare Hare*, and connect with God. The joy and satisfaction one feels in our heart is Krishna. This state is *yoga-sthah* (BG 2.48) and one can be sure of the presence of

Krishna and His guidance in our activities. In this way one will be 24/7 (*ananya cetasa*) in spiritual consciousness. There may be difficulties sometimes, but one shall nicely overcome them. By the mercy of Lord Krishna everything will be great. Difficulties (spiritual and material) will only make one better devotees, like steel is forged by annealing. Remember: devotees have challenges, not problems.

One becomes Krishna conscious by devotion only. By mental speculation one cannot understand the Supreme Spirit, because the mind is material. By serving Krishna with deep affection, one connects with Krishna, and the Lord gradually reveals Himself (*"bhaktya mam abhijanati"*—BG 18.55). One comes to know God as a person with His infinite attributes such as knowledge, beauty, wisdom, mercy, fame, and renunciation. One also gets showered by His mercy. Our lives become perfect and blissful. One becomes opulent, knowledgeable, wise and serene, and sees everything with great clarity; one becomes enlightened. With the happy presence of Krishna, one succeeds in whatever activity one is doing, be it reading, writing, working, cooking or cleaning. If one is awake in Krishna consciousness all one's work is perfect.

One should keep oneself in Krishna thoughts. Lord Krishna says in *The Bhagavad Gita* (18.65, 2.61, 10.9, 18.66), *"man-manā bhava mad-bhakto," "mat-parah," "mac-citta mad-gata-prana,"* and *"mam ekam saranam vraja,"* (fix your mind on me, become my devotee, become absorbed in me, think of me, meditate on me, take refuge in me). When one sleeps thinking of Krishna, one will have nice dreams. When one works, if one says Hare Krishna, one's work will be done nicely. When one eats *prasadam*, if one thinks of Krishna, one will feel happy, because one's mind will be clear. The more one chants *Krishna, Krishna*, the more one will be established in one's pure state (*svarupa*). One becomes anxiety free and clear headed. When one understands that one is part and parcel of Krishna, one is in one's constitutional position; what is there to worry about? One is dovetailed with Krishna, one is in Krishna, one is safe and one is happy.

The more one reads *The Bhagavad Gita*, the more insights spring up, the more one understands and one develops faith in Krishna. One realizes that it is all true (*"sarvam etad rtam manye"*—BG 10.14) like Arjuna. One becomes convinced that Krishna consciousness is the right way of living. One begins to know one's actual self (the soul, or *dehi*/indweller of the body). This is the beginning of knowledge. Without knowing one's true self, whatever knowledge one acquires, material or spiritual, will be flawed because one will be in the mode of ignorance. Our real life begins when one realizes one is a spirit soul, part and parcel of Krishna and acts according to Krishna's instructions (BG 3.31).

All things and beings are contained in the Cosmic Body of God (BG 11.13). We are parts and parcels of Krishna and our constitutional position is to serve Krishna (as a part's duty is to serve the whole or the finger's duty is to serve the body, nothing else). Our actual position is to serve our dear Lord Krishna (CC Madhya 20.108). To love and serve Krishna is only natural as we are born of Him.

By chanting the Maha Mantra (*Hare Krishna, Hare Krishna, Krishna Krishna, Hare Hare, Hare Rama, Hare Rama, Rama Rama, Hare Hare*), our body, mind and intelligence will be pure; our perception and understanding of material and spiritual worlds will be clear; and our miseries will disappear. If we chant the Holy Names, study or hear *The Srimad Bhagavad Gita*, perform deity worship and partake of *prasadam* we will quickly become enlightened. If we just chant or only make effort in one aspect of bhakti yoga, our progress will be slower. The more effort we put into the process of Krishna consciousness, the deeper we will dive into the ocean of bhakti-rasa nectar.

When one commits oneself to Krishna consciousness, one quickly becomes a *sadhu* (BG 9.31). Lord Sri Krishna is very favourable to saintly persons. He takes care of all their needs. He fills them with love, light and joy. He descends on earth on their account. He protects them and enjoys their association. All beings and things are but part and parcel of Krishna. Thus He is very much involved in the welfare of every being and everything. The universe functions by Sanatana Dharma or Krishna's order. If there is discrepancy in *dharma*, God Himself descends or sends His representative (BG 4.7–8). Lord Krishna makes everything normal again so that devotees can serve Him nicely and He can enjoy His universe.

The more one studies Krishna lila (retellings of His life), the more one studies *The Bhagavad Gita*, the more one becomes absorbed in Krishna *bhavana mrita* (thought) and one's life becomes like Krishna's life; one attains one's eternal and blissful existence. By knowing Krishna, one knows everything (BG 15.15). Above all, one develops love for Krishna, which is the ultimate goal of life. On the battlefield of Kurukeshetra, Lord Krishna bestowed Krishna consciousness on Arjuna by giving the knowledge of *The Bhagavad Gita*. Arjuna would be victorious anyway because he was fighting evil and injustice on the field of Truth (Dharma Kshetra) and most importantly, Lord Krishna was his charioteer. However, when he saw his relatives and revered personalities such as Bhisma, Drona and others on the opposing side, he became confused as to what the right action should be. He felt deep compassion in his heart and thought that doing his duty of fighting as a *kshatria* (warrior) was meaningless and unethical. He then became deeply sorrowful and decided not to fight.

Lord Sri Krishna, in His infinite mercy, gave Arjuna the transcendental knowledge (or royal knowledge) of Krishna consciousness. The Lord told distraught Arjuna that you are not your body; you are spirit (BG 2.13) and you should act as such. You should rise above the three modes of material nature, which are causes of pain and pleasure, by performance of yoga and being in Krishna consciousness (BG 2.46–48). In Krishna consciousness, all dualities or conflicting ideas are dissolved, and one acts in perfect harmony with nature or the cosmic law (Sanatana Dharma which emanates from Krishna). One can attain Krishna consciousness by the nine processes of bhakti (*sravanam, kirtanam, Vishnu smaranam, pada sevanam, archanam, vandanam, dasyam, sakhyam and atma nivedanam*). For this age of Kali, Lord Sri Krishna Chaitanya Mahaprabhu gave us the sublime method of chanting the Hare Krishna Maha Mantra, because Krishna is non-different from His name as Krishna is Absolute. We become Krishna conscious simply by chanting Hare Krishna.

Krishna consciousness is our ground state of being, which is also called *Bodhi citta* (Buddha mind), Christ consciousness or cosmic consciousness. It is the potential field of all thoughts, emotions, activity and creation (*kshetra*). It is the unified field of everything, material and spiritual. There is total harmony, balance and interconnectedness. By practicing bhakti yoga when we become Krishna conscious, our lives become automatically perfect and we become successful beyond our dreams. Hearing *The Bhagavad Gita* from Lord Krishna, Prince Arjuna became established in yoga, *yoga-sthah* (BG 2.48) or Krishna consciousness. He was also called Dhananjaya (winner of wealth). Thus he was also promised success as stated in the last verse of *The Bhagavad Gita* (opulence, victory, extraordinary power and morality, BG 18.78).

Prince Arjuna's mind became pure by reverently hearing (*sravanam*). His dilemma resulting from a conflict between duty and compassion became resolved; his mind switched from ordinary consciousness to Krishna consciousness; he became fully enlightened. There was no more duality or differentiation in his thinking and feeling. He was in harmony with every being and everything in the cosmos. He became the most ethical person. Now, being in Krishna consciousness, he would do the right action spontaneously. Every impulse of his consciousness would be identical with the impulse of cosmic consciousness or Krishna consciousness.

When one's mind is calm and pure sometimes one accesses one's original consciousness, which is eternal, full of knowledge, love, compassion, clarity and joy. However, one's ordinary consciousness is limited and one is only aware of one's own body. By yoga one can connect oneself with the entire universe and become cosmic conscious or Krishna conscious. This cosmic consciousness or field is the repository of all the things there are and are yet to be. This cosmic field contains the manifestations of all things and also the potential of all possibilities. This is full of all opulences: *aisvarya* (wealth), *virya* (power), *yasha* (fame), *sriya* (beauty), *jnana* (knowledge), *vairagya* (detachment) and many, many more. Although Lord Krishna is the possessor of all opulences, He is also detached from them because He is complete and full of pleasure (*atmarama*). By bhakti yoga one can be in transcendental consciousness and realize one's godlike nature. Qualitatively one will have all the opulences Krishna (God) has, but quantitatively they will be finite (*achintya-bheda-abheda*). One will truly realize that one is the image of God (*manasa jata*, born of the mind) and one is perfect.

Without Krishna consciousness no one can be happy because our constitutional position (*svarupa*) is to become Krishna conscious. One may become rich or famous or a scholar, but one cannot be happy without Krishna consciousness. Happiness comes when one transcends Maya or the three modes of material nature (*"mam eva ye prapadyante"*—BG 17.14). That's why it is imperative for us to practice bhakti yoga and be situated in Krishna consciousness (*yoga-sthah* or *Samadhistha*) by transcending the three *guna*s.

One endures the scorching heat of material life in *tapasya* to purify our existence (*tapa*) and attain divine life. Without becoming pure, one cannot become integrated with Krishna because He is supremely pure.

Our human life is meant for *tapasya* (voluntary or involuntary hardships). *Tapa divyam* is essential for spiritual life. Austerity or *tapasya* purifies our existence and thus qualifies us for bhakti yoga. By being immersed in yoga bhakti (*yoga-sthah*, transcendental consciousness) in a purified state we understand that we are part and parcel of Krishna. In chemical terms, we become fully miscible. In that state one is happy and blissful; one is in our original position. A child is perfectly happy only when he is with parents at home. Similarly one is also truly happy in Goloka Vrindavana with Krishna, which is our true home.

Lord Sri Krishna said (BG 13.1–2) that our body is the field (*kshetra*) and our soul is the knower of the field (*kshetrajna*). Our body is like a farmer's field and one can grow anything, both good and bad. The field has the potential for wonderful plants, but it must be cultivated and the correct seeds sown. Actually, the cosmos is another field and the knower of that field is Paramatma or Krishna. We only know our own body, but Lord Krishna is aware of the entire universe including our minute bodies. In our bodies, therefore, we have two *kshetrajnas*, the soul and the Supersoul, like two birds in the same tree. Our pure self is a part and parcel of Krishna; our duty is to serve Him.

A devotee of the Lord always remembers Krishna. By thinking of Krishna, without deviation, one always remains in transcendental consciousness. One's choice is always Krishna and not Maya (the three modes of material nature and sense gratification). A devotee knows that one is an integral part of the universe; one must always be in harmony with the cosmos. Thus serving Krishna is sine qua non, imperative. One must develop love for God, all living entities and the entire creation. To develop love for Krishna, one must diligently study *The Srimad Bhagavatam*, *The Bhagavad Gita*, *The Chaitanya Charitamrita* and other scriptures. *The Sri Chaitanya Charitamrita* (Madhya 22.8) says, "*sadhu sanga nama kirtana Bhagavad sravanam Mathura basa Sri Murtira sraddaya sevanam.*" A devotee should associate with other devotees, chant the Holy Names, hear *The Srimad Bhagavatam* and other scriptures, stay in a holy place like Mathura and perform deity worship with deep attention.

A devotee should engage his mind and senses (*hrtatmano hrtapranams ca*) while performing deity worship. Without this transcendental knowledge of the *shastras*, one's progress in realization of Krishna consciousness won't be perfect, and one's Krishna conscious activity or devotional service won't be perfect either. The more one knows about Lord Krishna and His pastimes, the more one will develop love for Him. By studying (*svadhyaya*) and bhakti yoga one removes all material contaminations, becomes pure and fully engages in bhakti yoga without deviation (*ananya bhak*, only remembering Krishna and nothing else). A devotee is a spiritual being having a material experience (*samsara*); by unflinching devotion to Krishna one regains one's original nature.

The perspective and conduct of an enlightened person is genuinely cosmic, because one is a part and parcel of the Cosmic Whole or Lord Sri Krishna. One is in tune with the Cosmic Mind. Anything one thinks or does is in harmony with the universe. There is no planning; one's thoughts and actions happen as a part of the cosmic working, like those of the sun and the moon, the stars, the ocean and the wind. One performs the right actions spontaneously, in harmony with the cosmos.

One can gradually raise one's consciousness to transcendental or Krishna consciousness by following bhakti yoga. By chanting the Holy Names one progressively purifies oneself and realizes that one is not the body, but rather spirit soul. By this understanding one becomes free of all material constraints, such as birth, death, old age and disease. A pure devotee exhibits the following qualities: charity (*dana*), good conduct (*sila*), forgiveness (*ksanti*), heroism (*virya*), meditation (*dhyana*), and wisdom (*prajna*). One becomes established in our pure original nature (*svarupa*). One's life becomes sublime and successful. One behaves and exists as cosmic entities. There is no anxiety, fear or worry. One's life blossoms like the flowers in the spring. One exists in Krishna consciousness; Krishna exists in us.

That is the ultimate success.

The Light of the Gita

Om Namo Bhagavate Vasudevaya.

The Srimad Bhagavad Gita is an extraordinary and celestial work of literature. It was spoken by the Supreme Person (Purushottama), or God Himself. It is eternal and the Absolute Truth, as it is from Krishna. To understand *The Bhagavad Gita*, one must be a devotee and friend of Krishna (*"bhakto 'si me sakha ceti"*—BG 4.3) like Arjuna was, otherwise it will remain a mystery (*rahasya*). No one can understand *The Bhagavad Gita* unless one chants and becomes a devotee of Lord Sri Krishna. One can grasp the essence of *The Bhagavad Gita* by the mercy of Lord Sri Krishna Chaitanya Mahaprabhu, who is Krishna Himself, and who gave the benediction of the Holy Name for this age.

The Bhagavad Gita elucidates five topics: the soul, Supersoul, karma, material nature and time. God (Parabrahman) is the underlying cosmic existence which is unborn, eternal and permanent, and who is the Controller of everything in the universe. The soul is but a part of God, the same in quality, but different in quantity. The soul pervades the material body and the Supersoul pervades the entire cosmos. Material nature is the external energy of God under the three modes: *sattva*, *raja* and *tama*. Karma is the activity of the living entities. Universal dissolution and manifestation occur under the purview of time. By understanding *The Srimad Bhagavad Gita*, one becomes Krishna conscious like Arjuna.

The Bhagavad Gita takes place on the battle field of Kurukeshetra where the Pandavas and Kauravas were prepared to battle. As the battle was about to commence, Arjuna asked Lord Sri Krishna to place his chariot in between the opposing armies. When he saw the fight would be with his relatives, friends and teachers, he became overcome with grief. He thought the consequence of the war would be catastrophic. Millions of people would die, and after that, society would collapse. As a result mankind would become uncivilized and immoral and descend into darkness. The gain from the conflict would be minimal, even if he were to win the war. He said to Lord Krishna that he would not fight.

Arjuna was talking from a material or bodily concept of life. Lord Krishna told him that our true nature is spiritual. All living entities are actually souls and are encased in the material body; their souls are unborn (*aja*, no death), permanent (*nitya*, constant), eternal (*sasvata*, no decay) and ancient (*purana*, ageless). The soul takes on a new body as people put on new clothes, discarding the old ones. In fact, Arjuna would not be killing anybody; in the battle, only the material bodies would perish. The embodied beings forget about their true nature when they take on their material bodies. The soul of the universe, Lord Krishna, remembers everything because He does not go through *janma*, *mrityu*, *jara* and *vyadhi* (birth, death, old age and disease) like ordinary living entities. A *jiva* can however extricate themself from material nature by bhakti yoga, by linking with the Supreme Self. If one is too attached to material nature, one does not have the determination or the power to perform yoga. If one is disciplined and one performs bhakti yoga, one's intelligence becomes steady and divine. One thus understands one's spiritual nature and one's relationship with God. One understands how to conduct oneself in this material world so that one performs material duties while performing devotional service (dovetailing material activities with spiritual activities).

Everything in the cosmos emanates from Lord Vāsudeva (Krishna) and everything belongs to Him. One's constitutional position is that of a servitor; when one sincerely serves Krishna one gets rewarded. One should do one's work as a duty and shouldn't enjoy the fruits of labour. Prince Arjuna knew that his duty was to fight, but he became overcome with compassion. It is a rare case when one's duty and feelings are in opposition.

Lord Krishna (BG 2.48) advised him to be in transcendental or Krishna consciousness: *"yoga-sthah kuru karmani."* At this level one's consciousness is in total harmony. One's thinking and feelings are integrated. One is automatically guided to the right activity. In Krishna consciousness one becomes *sthita prajna* or a person of steady wisdom. Lord Krishna's revelation is the key to going through life's choices correctly. Thus by knowing oneself as a soul and not the body, and conducting oneself in transcendental consciousness one can make one's life perfect and successful. The mind of a person in transcendental consciousness is centered on Krishna. One's speech and activities are at once directly and indirectly related to Krishna. A devotee's mind and senses are fully absorbed in Krishna. One only talks about Krishna, and one roams in the material world like a lion, without being attracted to sense gratification. One is steady, self-controlled and decisive. Like a tortoise, one uses the senses when needed, and retracts them when not required. The vision of Lord Krishna, even in a dream, transforms one's consciousness to transcendental consciousness and one's mode of life changes. One obtains a higher taste or transcendental taste for everything. To keep oneself steady, one should practice devotional service, especially *japa* of the Hare Krishna Maha Mantra, which is recommended for this age. One should chant the Holy Name of Krishna, eat *prasadam* and worship the Lord.

To live in the world one must do both spiritual and material work; both are necessary to be successful, as karma emanates from Brahma or God. If one only meditates, one's physical body and mind will degrade. If only engages in material activity, one will become animalistic (eating, sleeping, defending and mating); no higher consciousness will be possible. One must therefore meditate on Krishna and perform one's worldly duties such as cooking, cleaning, reading, writing, counting, defending and farming, being absorbed in the thought of Krishna. Work done as a sacrifice to Vishnu must be performed; otherwise work causes bondage to the material world. The fruits of all work should be offered to Krishna. One's food should also be offered to Krishna. Thus one's work and food will be spiritualized and one will progress towards spiritual life; that is, one will know one's true nature and one's relationship with God. When one is in full Krishna consciousness, one transcends the three modes of material nature; one does not have any duty to perform. However, one should work in order to teach other people. God also works to maintain the world. Therefore one should not shy away from work. For a devotee, working for the Lord is a transcendental pleasure.

Arjuna wished to know from the Lord why people engage in sinful activities. The Lord replied that *kama* or lust (sitting in the senses, the mind and intelligence) impels a person, sometimes unwillingly, to commit offences. However, being in pure consciousness, one can overcome lust and avoid committing any sinful activities. One should chant the Holy Names, read *The Bhagavad Gita*, eat *prasadam* and be self-realized.

Previously Lord Krishna gave the science of Krishna consciousness to the sun god, though the knowledge was lost in the course of time. Lord Krishna gave this Brahma *vidya* to Arjuna again in Dvapara Yuga, about 5,000 years ago. Again, this knowledge was lost, and in our current age, Lord Krishna appeared as Lord Sri Krishna Chaitanya Mahaprabhu to revive this knowledge and asked people to chant the Hare Krishna Maha Mantra (*Hare Krishna, Hare Krishna, Krishna Krishna, Hare Hare, Hare Rama, Hare Rama, Rama Rama, Hare Hare*). Lord Sri Krishna Chaitanya Mahaprabhu also said that Krishna is the Supreme Master and living entities are His servants (*vritya*). The four pillars of *dharma* are: *tapa, shaucha, daya, satyam*. Whenever there is a discrepancy in the performance of *dharma*, God advents on earth and sets everything in order again.

In Dvapara Yuga the Lord descended on earth at the requrest of Bhumi Devi (Mother Earth) because the burden of the demons was too hard to bear. In Kali Yuga, the Lord made a special appearance as Sri Krishna Chaitanya Mahaprabhu at the request of Sri Advaita Acharya to give mankind an easy means to be delivered. Also, when one chants the Holy Name of the

Lord, then Lord Krishna appears in the heart of the devotee. He protects and illumines the heart.

A devotee who knows the science of Krishna and His *lila* becomes free from all material entanglement and goes back to Vaikuntha (the spiritual world). One should be absorbed in transcendental consciousness and not let the mind be deflected from the Lord's lotus feet. Worshipping demigods is not beneficial, as doing so causes one to come back to the material world—although one may enjoy an opulent life. But they will still be subjected to the four miseries.

The entire material creation is under the three modes or *guna*s. Humans under the spell of *sattva*, *raja* and *tama* become divided into four classes, namely *brahmana*, *kshatria*, *vaisya* and *sudra*. God is transcendental to these modes and so are His devotees (being in the *hamsa* or swanlike class). If one acts in Krishna consciousness, one's activities are free of reaction. If one does not perform one's duty (Krishna consciousness), but does something else (Maya), one gets a reaction. In all *yugas*, the material world is under the three *guna*s, and thus the living entities will undergo the threefold miseries (self-inflicted pain, pain inflicted by other living entities and natural disasters inflicted by Mother Nature). Thus there will always be war, pestilence and famine. Because there will always be misery in the material world, a devotee should not be disturbed by them and should keep his focus on Krishna. One cannot help others if disturbed and overwhelmed by the misery of the world. Walt Whitman has predicted that people will become brothers and sisters in the future.

A person fully absorbed in Krishna consciousness is sure to attain the spiritual kingdom. Her activities are spiritualized. Whatever one does being in Krishna consciousness is *yajna* (sacrifice). The best sacrifice is *japa*. Attaining knowledge is also a great sacrifice, because it destroys ignorance. Without knowledge, we cannot be proper devotees. We will make many mistakes. We will fumble through life. We won't know what to do, what not to do, or how to do. Our devotional life will be imperfect. One can offer hearing (Krishna katha) breathing (kriya yoga or *pranayama*) or study of the *shastras* (*svadhyaya*) as *yajna*. By such processes one can be immersed in thought of Krishna and be free of sin. The best process of *yajna* for this age is the chanting of the Holy Name. Regardless of one's current *guna* and karma one can attain all perfections and go back to Krishna at the end of one's life.

Although a self-realized person has no duty and is situated in transcendental knowledge, it is beneficial for a devotee to be active. Without a healthy body and mind it is hard to be fully engaged in bhakti yoga. Living entities are by nature active. If one controls one's senses, including the mind, and offers the results of one's activities to the Lord, then one is not implicated in the material world and is happy in transcendental consciousness.

All the activities of this body are carried out by the senses under the modes of material nature. The soul is only the enlivening energy and does nothing. When one's intelligence, mind, faith and shelter are all fixed at the lotus feet of Krishna, one sees all living entities, be they a *brahmana*, an elephant, a cat or a dog with equal vision. An intelligent person doesn't take part in material pleasures of the senses, as they are the source of misery. One who is self-situated (not in body or ego) is happy and a perfect mystic. If a person is fully conscious of Lord Krishna, offers all one's work as *yajna*, and knows that God is a well-wisher and benefactor of all *jivas*, such a person attains peace (the ground state of being—an unperturbed state).

Lord Krishna said that one who is unattached to the fruits of one's work and works as one is obligated is a true yogi or mystic. "Yoga" means to "yolk" or link oneself with the Supreme. To be a yogi one must give up desires for sense gratification, including that of the mind. One can elevate oneself or degrade oneself by one's mind. Bhakti does not grow if one does not give up sense gratification. One should make one's mind a friend by practicing bhakti yoga.

To discipline the mind and the senses, one should sit in meditation in a quiet place such as a deity room, and focus the mind on Krishna. He is known as Shyamasundara, with peacock feathers in His hair, a flute in His hand, dressed in a yellow *dhoti* wearing a long flower garland around His neck. By continuous practice of *dhyana* one's mind becomes serene, one enjoys the nectar of bhakti to the Supreme Lord and one transcends material existence. There is no greater gain than attaining this state. One should be moderate in all activities and use one's intelligence to keep oneself established in *samadhi* or God consciousness. A true yogi observes Lord Krishna in all beings and all beings in Him. A devotee sees equally the beauty of all beings and is deeply compassionate to all living entities.

Arjuna said that meditation is a difficult a task, because controlling the mind is as impossible as controlling the wind. Lord Krishna replied that one cannot be self-realized with an unbridled mind. An enlightened person's mind is like a steady flame in a windless place. One can gradually bring one's mind under control by chanting and meditation. Even if a person doesn't fully succeed in self-realization, one will continue one's practice in one's next life, from the point of achievement where one left off. There is no loss of the transcendental benefit of self-realization and other spiritual merits.

Lord Krishna said that Arjuna can know Him in full by being absorbed in the thought of Krishna and practicing bhakti or devotion. Success in God realization is rare; perhaps one in many thousands succeeds and becomes perfected (*siddha*). In our current Kali Yuga however, by the mercy of Lord Sri Krishna Chaitanya Mahaprabhu, one can be self-realized by chanting the Maha Mantra: *Hare Krishna, Hare Krishna, Krishna Krishna, Hare Hare, Hare Rama, Hare Rama, Rama Rama, Hare Hare.*

All things emanate from Krishna; He is the Original Creator. The sun, the moon, the earth, the stars and the galaxies, everything rests upon Him (Paramatma) as pearls are strung on a thread. God is the taste of water, the light of the sun and the moon, and the cosmic sound "om."

Four kinds of pious people take to spiritual life: the distressed (*arta*), the desirer of wealth (*artharthi*), the inquisitive (*jijnasu*), and the wise (*jnani*). Of those, the wise who are naturally engaged in devotion are the dearest to Lord Krishna. Some people, knowing Krishna as the origin of everything (Vāsudeva), surrender to Him and are called *mahatmas*. The unwise and unintelligent people worship demigods because Maya deludes them. The worshippers of demigods do not attain Krishna consciousness; they go to the planets of the demigods. The devotees of the Lord go to Goloka Vrindavana.

Arjuna was curious to know what Brahman, *adhyatma*, *adhibhuta*, *adhidaiva* and *adhiyajna* are. He also wanted to know what karma is and how one can remember Krishna at the time of death. The indestructible eternal substratum of existence is Brahman or Parabrahman. The individual living entity is *adhyatma* or the soul. Brahman or Vāsudeva is the ultimate reality and our soul or *atman* is a part of it. The action of all living beings is karma. All living entities together as a whole, are known as *adhibhuta*. All the demigods like the sun and the moon, Indra and Varuna, are part of the Visvarupa of God, called *adhidaiva*. Lord Krishna residing in all beings is the enjoyer of all sacrifices (*yajna* or offerings) and is known as *adhiyajna*. The actions pertaining to individual living entities is karma, and one can remember Krishna at the time of death by practicing bhakti yoga.

The best practice for Kali Yuga is chanting of the Maha Mantra: *Hare Krishna, Hare Krishna, Krishna Krishna, Hare Hare, Hare Rama, Hare Rama, Rama Rama, Hare Hare*. One should strive to remember Krishna's name always while performing all activities, even resting, which will ensure that one remembers Krishna at the time of death. If one remembers the Lord at the time of death, one goes back to Krishna Loka (Goloka Vrindavana); therefore, one should always remember Krishna and do one's duty. One should never worship gods like Brahma, Indra, or Vayu, because they are part of material nature. If one goes to their planets by pious activities, one will live there for a long time, but in the end, will go through repeated birth and death and attain no liberation.

A day of Brahma equals 4.2 billion years. There are many *maha yuga* cycles in that time span. A *maha yuga* is made up of Kali Yuga (432,000 years), Dvapara Yuga (864,000 years), Treta Yuga (1,296,000 years) and Satya Yuga (1,728,000 years). According to Swami Sri Yuteshwar, there is a smaller *yuga* cycle corresponding to the earth's axial precession within each *maha yuga* (composed of 24,000 years). In this smaller *yuga*, Kali Yuga is 1,200 years, Dvapara Yuga is 2,400 years, Treta Yuga is 3,600 years and Satya yuga is 4,800 years. There is an upward and downward cycle composed of 12,000 years each in the smaller *yuga* cycle, like a sinusoidal wave. Lord Sri Krishna was born on 21st July 3,227 B.C. and the Mahabharata war was on 22nd November 3067 B.C. At the moment we are in the larger Kali Yuga of 432,000 years, and 318 years into Dvapara Yuga within the smaller cycle, which is now ascending. Lord Sri Krishna Chaitanya Mahaprabhu was born on 18th February 1486, which was at the end of the smaller Kali Yuga and provided some relief. As Lord Krishna says (BG 4.8), He descends age after age. There is no time and age, no matter how dark, where Krishna and/or his pure disciples are not present in His material creation.

A devotee's life is beyond the influence of time, the material modes, the *yugas* or the alignment of the planets. A devotee always lives anxiety-free, as if in Vaikuntha, and at the end of life goes back to Goloka Vrindavana. The devotee does not need to worry about being born or dying at a particular time or in a particular *yuga*. The devotee is always under the protection of Lord Sri Krishna. For example, Bhisma, the grandsire of the Pandavas and Kauravas, waited on a bed of arrows at the end of the Kurukeshetra war to leave his body at an auspicious time when the sun began its northern passage, because he was not a devotee, although very pious.

On the battlefield of Kurukeshetra Lord Krishna bestowed the royal knowledge, royal secret upon Arjuna. What is this royal knowledge or royal secret? It is the knowledge of Krishna consciousness; it is knowing that I am not the body but a spirit soul (*aham Brahmasmi*); a part and parcel of the Supersoul, Lord Sri Krishna. I am simultaneously and inconceivably one and different (*achintya-bheda-abheda tattva*); thus, my eternal duty is to serve Krishna. I am in the body, so the body and the mind must be utilized in the service of the Supreme Person. I should always be absorbed in Krishna consciousness and all my activities should be performed in that state.

By Krishna consciousness one can attain the abode of Lord Krishna. A faithless person, even in the mode of goodness, is caught in the cycle of birth and death. The entire cosmic order is under Lord Krishna and by His will it is manifested and annihilated again and again. Fools deride the Lord thinking that He is an ordinary human being, as they do not know His transcendental nature. The works and culture of these demonic people, however great they seem, are totally meaningless. Those who don't know the transcendental nature of Lord Sri Krishna will not become Krishna conscious. Devotees always sing the glories of the Lord (*Hare Krishna, Hare Krishna, Krishna Krishna, Hare Hare, Hare Rama, Hare Rama, Rama Rama, Hare Hare*) being under His protection. Lord Krishna is the father, mother, the support and the grandsire of the universe. He is the goal, the sustainer, maintainer, eternal witness and the dearmost friend of all living entities. The Lord takes care of His devotees, whatever need there may be. At the end of life, a devotee goes to Krishna Loka, unlike the demigod and ancestor worshippers who go to those minor heavens. Worshippers of Lord Krishna will live with Him.

Lord Krishna accepts a leaf, a flower, a fruit or a little water, if offered with love. Whatever one does, eats, offers or gives away, and whatever austerity (*tapa*) one performs, one should offer it to Krishna. In this way, one can free oneself from karma and sin and be liberated. No one is barred from devotional service to the Lord, whoever they are. One should think of Krishna, become His devotee by the nine processes of bhakti, offer obeisance and worship Him. By being absorbed in Krishna consciousness one will surely go to Krishna Loka.

Lord Krishna is the Supreme God or Bhagavan. He is unborn and beginningless. He is the source of all living entities, gods and everything material and spiritual. Intelligence, knowledge, forgiveness, truthfulness, sense control, happiness, nonviolence, satisfaction, fame, and other good qualities emanate from Him.

Brahma, the Seven Sages (Vasishta, Marichi, Angirasa, Atri, Pualsthya, Pulaaha and Krathu), and all the Manus come from God's mind. The pure devotees always think of Krishna. Krishna gives them knowledge by which they go to Him. Arjuna understood that Lord Krishna is Parabrahman Himself. Arjuna said that he totally accepted as truth all that Lord Krishna told him. He wished to know how to constantly remember Him. He asked Krishna to tell him in detail about all His opulences as he never tires of hearing nectarean words about Krishna. Lord Krishna said He would only tell Arjuna of a few of His prominent manifestations, because His opulence is limitless.

Lord Krishna said that He is present in the heart of all beings as the Supersoul: Of the Adityas, I am Vishnu, of the luminaries, I am the radiant sun, of the winds, I am Marichi, and among the stars, I am the moon. Of the Vedas, I am the Sama Veda, among gods I am Indra and of the senses, I am the mind and in living beings, I am consciousness. Of the Rudras, I am Shiva, of the Yakshas, I am Kuvera, of the Vasus, I am Agni and of mountains, I am Meru. Of priests, I am Brihaspati, of generals, I am Kartikeya, of bodies of water, I am the ocean, of the great sages, I am Bhrigu. Of vibrations, I am *om*, of *yajnas*, I am the chanting of the Holy Names, or *japa*, and of immovable things, I am the Himalayas. Among the Daityas, I am the devoted Prahlada, among subduers, I am time, among animals, I am the lion, among the birds, I am Garuda. Of purifiers, I am the wind, of wielders of weapons, I am Sri Rama, of fishes, I am *makara* (the shark) and among the rivers, I am the Ganga. Of the descendants of Vrisni, I am Vāsudeva Krishna, of the Pandavas, I am Arjuna and of the sages, I am Vyasadeva, compiler of the Vedas.

Lord Krishna is the generating seed of all existence. No being, moving or unmoving, can exist without Him. There is no end of His magnificent manifestations or *vibhuti*. All opulent, beautiful and glorious creations spring from Him and are but sparks of His splendour. With a single fragment of Himself, the Lord pervades and supports the entire cosmos.

Arjuna said that after hearing Lord Krishna's instructions about the most confidential spiritual subjects, his illusions were dispelled. Arjuna was glad Lord Krishna described His different cosmic manifestations and he felt curious to see His universal form. Lord Krishna said that yes, you can see My cosmic form composed of hundreds and thousands of varied, divine and multicoloured forms. But Arjuna couldn't see them with his material eyes, so Lord Krishna gave him divine eyes to behold His mystic opulence.

After having spoken thus, Lord Krishna, who is Yogeshvara, showed His universal form with unlimited mouths, unlimited eyes and unlimited wonderful visions. The form was decorated with many celestial ornaments and many divine upraised weapons. This Vishnu form wore celestial garlands and garments, and divine scents emanated from His body. It all was wondrous, brilliant, infinite and all expanding, as if thousands of suns rose at once into the sky; such was the effulgence of this mighty form. At that time Arjuna could see the unlimited expansion of the Lord in one place, although divided into many parts. Arjuna prayed (BG 11.18, 20, 22), "You are the ultimate resting place of all this universe. You are inexhaustible, and You are the oldest. You are the maintainer of the eternal religion ... Although You are one, You spread throughout the sky and the planets and all space between ... Lord Śiva, the Ādityas, the Vasus, the Sādhyas, the Viśvedevas, the two Aśvīs, the Maruts, the forefathers, the Gandharvas, the Yakṣas, the Asuras and the perfected demigods are beholding You in wonder."

Seeing this mighty form of Lord Krishna with His many radiant colours, His gaping mouths and glowing eyes, Arjuna's mind became perturbed with fear. He saw all his enemies, kings, soldiers, along with Bhisma, Drona and Karna rushing into His fearsome mouths. Fearful Arjuna asked the Lord who He was and what His mission was. Lord Krishna replied that He is *kala*, or time, the destroyer of the worlds, and He had come to destroy everyone except the Pandavas. He also said that all Arjuna's enemies were already dead, and Arjuna should be but an instrument of Krishna.

After hearing this, Arjuna offered obeisance to the Lord with folded hands again and again. He said (BG 11.36, 38), "O Hrisikesha, the world becomes joyful hearing Your Name, and thus everyone becomes attached to You. The devotees offer respects to You ... You are the knower of everything, and You are all that is knowable. You are the supreme refuge, above the material modes. O limitless form! This whole cosmic manifestation is pervaded by You!"

Arjuna realized that Lord Krishna is Bhagavan, and felt embarrassed that he had addressed Krishna as "O Yadava, O my friend," unknowingly. He asked for forgiveness for dishonouring Him. There is no one greater than Lord Krishna and He should be worshipped by every living being.

Arjuna asked Lord Krishna to withdraw the fearful cosmic form and show Himself in His familiar, four-armed form as Narayana. Lord Krishna obliged and then showed him first the Narayana form, and then His beautiful, two-armed Shyamasundara form. Lord Krishna said that even the demigods ever seek the opportunity to see Him in the Shyamasundara form, which means that Arjuna was still looking at Him with transcendental vision. No one can see the Lord in that form simply by studying the Vedas, by serious penances, charity or worship. This form can only be seen by undivided bhakti, as seen by Arjuna directly standing before Him. One who engages in pure bhakti yoga, free from fruitive activities and mental speculation, one who works for Him, and makes Him the supreme goal of life, and who is friendly to every living entity certainly goes to Lord Krishna.

Arjuna asked which path was better, bhakti yoga or worship of the impersonal Brahman. Lord Krishna said bhakti was certainly better, but those who follow the impersonal path will go to Brahman. The impersonal path is very troublesome for embodied beings, but those who worship Lord Krishna giving up all their activities are quickly delivered from the ocean of birth and death. One should just fix one's mind upon the Lord and engage all one's intelligence in Krishna, and then one will live in Krishna always. If one can't fix one's mind steadily on Krishna, then one should follow the regulative principles of bhakti yoga (*vaidhi bhakti*). Following *vaidhi bhakti* will lead to the development of pure bhakti. If one cannot follow *vaidhi bhakti*, then one should try to work for Krishna (for example preaching, building temples, cleaning the temple, writing and publishing work about Krishna). If one cannot work for Krishna, then one should give up the results of one's work and try to be self-situated. To be self-situated is to be egoless, be in one's constitutional position and consider oneself a servant of Krishna. If one cannot give up the results of one's work and be self-situated, then one should engage in the study of transcendental knowledge. Better than studying transcendental knowledge is meditation on Krishna, and better than meditation on Krishna is renunciation of the fruits of one's work for Krishna. All these steps lead to the development of pure bhakti to Lord Krishna.

When a person is not envious but is a kind friend to all living entities, doesn't think oneself a proprietor, is even minded, satisfied, self-controlled and engaged in bhakti yoga with determination, that person is very dear to Lord Krishna. One who follows this nectarean path of bhakti yoga and completely engages oneself with faith, making Lord Krishna the supreme goal is very, very dear to Lord Krishna.

Arjuna wished to know about *prakriti* (nature), *purusha* (the enjoyer), *kshetra* (the field), *kshetrajna* (the knower of the field), knowledge, and the object of knowledge. Lord Krishna replied that the body is the field, and the soul is the knower of the field. Lord Krishna, as the Supersoul, is the Knower in all bodies, and to understand the body and its knower (soul) is called knowledge. The five great elements (earth, water, fire, wind, ether), false ego, intelligence, the three modes of material nature, the 10 senses and the mind, the five sense objects (desire, hatred, happiness, distress, consciousness and convictions or *dhriti*), all constitute the field of activities and interactions. In short, the field of activities is the material world.

When a devotee advances in search of the Absolute Truth or Krishna, and as the devotee's knowledge grows, the devotee becomes humble, nonviolent, tolerant, simple, self-controlled, egoless, detached from the senses and the sense objects, and searches for a spiritual master or guru. The guru is the representative of Krishna and knows the science of Krishna (*"yei kṛṣṇa-tattva-vettā, sei guru haya"*—CC Madhya 8.128). Srila A. C. Bhaktivedanta Swami Prabhupada is the guru and proponent of bhakti yoga of the current age. He was instrumental in spreading the Holy Names in all towns and villages of the world as predicted by Sri Krishna Chaitanya Mahaprabhu. His devotees have constructed the *adbhuta mandir* in Mayapur, which was foretold by Sri Nityananda Prabhu.

The Supersoul is the original source of all senses. He is the maintainer of all living beings, He transcends the modes of material nature and He is the master of all three modes. Although the Supersoul appears to be divided among all beings and things, He is never divided. He is the source of light in all luminous objects. He is knowledge and He is also the object of knowledge. He is situated in everyone's heart and is the force that binds the nucleus of every atom.

Material nature and the living entities are beginningless. Their transformations and the modes of matter are products of material nature. The living entities in material nature enjoy the three modes, and because of their association with material nature, they meet with good and evil among various species. This is the process of reincarnation; depending on one's association with a particular *guna*, one may be born as a sage, philosopher, scientist, cat, dog, insect or a tree. Nevertheless, one does not get liberation, but the soul transmigrates from one body to another among various species to fulfill one's desires. The Supersoul exists in every body as the overseer and permitter.

When one becomes a devotee the Supersoul guides one to the correct action. Some perceive the Supersoul through meditation, some through cultivation of knowledge, and still others through working without fruitive desires. Again, there are others who worship the Supreme Person upon hearing about Him from others, such as chanting the Holy Names. They attain perfection and transcend the path of birth and death.

One who sees the Supersoul present everywhere, in every living being, doesn't degrade himself by his mind. He is a friend to all living beings. One who can see all activities are performed by the body, which is created of material nature, and sees that the self does nothing, actually sees. Krishna is the actual doer and master of everything. As the sun alone illuminates this entire universe, so does the soul illuminate the entire body, and the Supersoul pervades and illuminates the entire cosmos.

By becoming fixed in the knowledge of Krishna consciousness, one can attain transcendental nature, like that of Lord Sri Krishna (the same composition but in minute quantity, for example, H_2O or water is the same in a drop or in the ocean). Thus established, one is not born at the time of creation, or disturbed at the time of dissolution.

All living entities are born of material nature and Lord Krishna is the Supreme Father. Material nature consists of three modes, goodness (*sattva*), passion (*raja*) and ignorance (*tama*). When a living entity comes in contact with material nature, they become conditioned by these modes. The mode of goodness is illuminating and it frees one from sinful reactions. One becomes happy and intelligent. The mode of passion is born of unlimited desires and cravings and it binds one to fruitive actions. The mode of ignorance causes delusion of all embodied beings.

When one dies in the mode of goodness he attains to the higher planets of great sages. When one dies in the mode of passion one takes birth among those engaged in fruitive activities. When one dies in the mode of ignorance, one takes birth in the animal and plant kingdoms.

Activities done in the mode of goodness are pure, but activities in the mode of passion result in misery and activities performed in the mode of ignorance result in foolishness. From the mode of goodness, real knowledge develops; from the mode of passion greed develops and from the mode of ignorance, develops foolishness (being *hrita jnana* or bereft of knowledge), madness and illusion.

Those situated in the mode of goodness gradually go upward to the higher planets, those in the mode of passion live on the earthly planets, and those in the mode of ignorance go to hellish planets. A devotee of Lord Krishna is beyond the three modes of material nature. Simply by chanting the Holy Names and engaging in devotional service, one transcends the modes of material nature and becomes Krishnized.

Arjuna asked Lord Krishna (BG 14.21), "By which symptoms is one known who is transcendental to these three modes?"

Lord Krishna answered that when one is situated in the self and is even minded, treats friends and foes equally and has renounced all material activities, such a person is said to have transcended the modes of material nature. When one engages in bhakti yoga, one at once transcends the modes of material nature and comes to the level of immortal, imperishable Brahman; one becomes a pure devotee.

The Lord said that there is an imperishable banyan tree with its roots upward and branches downward and whose leaves are the Vedic hymns. The tree is nourished by the three modes of material nature, and the twigs are the objects of the senses. The tree represents the material world. Our human body is also an upside down tree, but smaller. The tree binds one to material nature. If one wishes to be free, one must develop detachment. This tree is a reflection of the spiritual world, and the reflection occurs in the river of desire or *kama*. The supreme abode of Krishna is self-effulgent, and the human tree is also self-illumined when the yogi raises one's consciousness to the topmost chakra (Sahasrara) at the crown of the head.

The living entities of this conditioned world are parts and parcels of Krishna, and they work hard for living with their six senses. Being parts and parcels of Krishna, the living entities' duty is to dovetail their consciousness with the Supreme consciousness, Krishna, and be engaged in devotional service to the Lord.

When a living entity transmigrates from one body to another, it carries different conceptions of life (via the subtle body which is composed of mind, intelligence and ego) along with the soul, as the air carries aromas. According to one's mindset and mode one obtains a certain type of body. For example, a person in the mode of goodness and of knowledge may be born as a sage, while a lusty person in the mode of ignorance may be born as a tree.

A devotee can understand the process of transmigration and can also clearly see the events and activities changing in material nature. The splendour of the sun, the moon and fire comes from Krishna. By Krishna's energy the planets stay in orbit. The moon, by its attraction, influences the life of the vegetables (by tidal forces and drawing water and nutrients to the plants' circulatory systems). Krishna is also the fire of digestion in all living entities and the air of life. The Lord is situated in everyone's heart and from Him comes remembrance, knowledge and forgetfulness. By all the Vedas, the Lord is to be known. One who knows Krishna as the Supreme Person is the knower of everything.

The devotee of the Lord has many transcendental qualities, such as fearlessness, purification of existence, cultivation of spiritual knowledge, charity, self-control, truthfulness, tranquility, compassion for all living entities, steady determination and many others. A devotee is godly and endowed with divine nature. Pride, arrogance, conceit, anger, harshness and ignorance belong to those of demonic nature. Lord Krishna assured Arjuna that he was born with divine qualities. Demonic people do not know what should be done and what should not be done. They are unclean, untruthful and they misbehave. Demonic people say the world is unreal and there is no God in control; they say the world is produced of sex desire. Demonic people are lost to themselves and have no intelligence. They engage in horrible works to destroy the world. They think to gratify the senses is the prime necessity of human civilization and their anxiety is immeasurable. Demonic people are envious and mischievous and they are cast into various demonic species of life. There are three gates leading to hell: lust, anger and greed. One should shun these and perform actions conducive to self-realization. One should follow scriptural injunctions so that one may be gradually elevated to higher consciousness.

Arjuna enquired of Krishna (BG 17.1), "What is the situation of those who do not follow the principles of scripture but worship according to their own imagination? Are they in goodness, in passion or in ignorance?"

Krishna replied (BG 17.2), "According to the modes of nature acquired by the embodied soul, one's faith (*shraddha*) can be of three kinds, in goodness, in passion or in ignorance."

People in the mode of goodness worship the demigods, those in the mode of passion worship demons, and those in the mode of ignorance worship ghosts and goblins. The demons, impelled by lust and desire, undergo severe penances not recommended by the scriptures.

People in the mode of goodness prefer *sattvic* food which increases the duration of life, purifies one's existence, and gives strength, health and satisfaction. Foods that are too bitter, too sour, salty, or hot and pungent are *rajasic* and liked by those in the mode of passion. Such foods cause distress and disease. *Tamasic* food is tasteless, rotten and untouchable. It is liked by those in the mode of ignorance.

Sacrifice performed according to the direction of the scripture, as a matter of duty, expecting no reward, is in the mode of goodness, but sacrifice performed for some material benefit or for the sake of pride, is in the mode of passion. Sacrifice done without regard for scriptural direction, and without distribution of *prasadam*, is in the mode of ignorance.

Austerity of the body consists of worshipping the Supreme Lord, the *brahmanas*, the spiritual master and superiors, like the father and mother. Austerity of the body also includes cleanliness (as it relates to *saucha*), simplicity (truth or *satyam*), celibacy or austerity (*tapas*) and nonviolence (*daya*).

Tapas (austerity), *saucha* (cleanliness), *daya* (compassion) and *satyam* (truth) are the four pillars of *dharma*. Austerity of speech in the mode of goodness consists of speaking words that are truthful and beneficial, reciting Vedic literature and chanting the Holy Names. Austerity of the mind, in the mode of goodness, consists of contentment, simplicity, gravity, self-control and purification of one's existence. Austerity performed in the mode of goodness is elevated to the transcendental platform when executed for the Supreme Lord Krishna. Charity given out of duty, without expectation of return, at the proper time and place, and to a worthy person, is considered to be in the mode of goodness. When one performs sacrifice, charity and penance, one should start with the sound "om" and end with *"om tat sat."*

When one gives up activities based on material desire, it is called *sannyasa*. Giving up the results of all activities is called *tyaga*. Acts of sacrifice, charity and penance must be performed because they purify even the great souls, and one's existence. All these activities should be performed without attachment and as a matter of duty. Prescribed duties should never be renounced. Giving up prescribed duties is being in the mode of ignorance. It is impossible for an embodied being to give up all activities, but one can renounce the fruits of action.

Actually, one should perform all activities, including sacrifice, charity and penance, for the satisfaction of Lord Krishna. One should not consider oneself the doer of activities, because the Supersoul or Krishna is the Doer. In the material world, the activities of all living entities are performed by the body, mind, speech or matter itself, and are under the control of the three modes of material nature. However, one can extricate oneself from these three modes by performing devotional service, especially hearing and chanting.

Knowledge, by which a person sees every living being as spirit souls, is in the mode of goodness. Knowledge by which one considers oneself the body, working very hard in this world, and destruction of the body as the end of existence, is in the mode of passion. Knowledge by which one thinks wealth and bodily comfort, such as eating, sleeping, defending and mating, is everything, and is lazy and greedy, is in the mode of ignorance.

Action which is regulated and performed without attachment and without desire for fruitive results is in the mode of goodness. Action performed with great effort for the satisfaction of gratifying one's desires and enacted from a sense of false ego, considering oneself the doer, is in the mode of passion. Action performed in delusion, disregarding scriptural injunctions, is in the mode of ignorance. This action causes destruction and distress.

One's understanding (*buddhi*) and determination (*dhriti*) are also according to the three modes of material nature. When a person knows what should be done and what should not be done, what is binding and what is liberating, that understanding is in the mode of goodness. When one's understanding cannot distinguish between *dharma* (religion) and a*dharma* (irreligion), the action that should be done and the action that should not be done, one is in the mode of passion. When one understands irreligion as religion, and strives in the wrong direction, doing what should not be done, that understanding is in the mode of ignorance. When a person's determination is unbreakable, and sustained by yoga practice and self-control, it is in the mode of goodness.

A person's happiness is in the mode of goodness when one awakens to self-realization (*atma buddhi*). That which in the beginning is like poison, but in the end is like nectar, is austerity and in the mode of goodness. (However, bhakti yoga, which is transcendental, is always pleasurable even from the beginning.) For example, studying the scriptures may be difficult at first, but is sublime in the end. On the other hand, happiness derived from the contact of the senses with their objects, which is pleasant at the beginning, but results in misery at the end, is in the mode of passion. And happiness which is blind to self-realization, which is delusive and arises from laziness and darkness, is in the nature of ignorance. There is no being that is not under the control of the three modes of material nature in this material world. However, anyone can transcend the modes of material nature by devotional service to the Lord.

By worship of the Lord, who is the source of all beings and is all-pervading, one can attain perfection through performing one's own work. All work is covered by some fault, just as fire is covered by smoke. By engaging in devotional service one can return to one's original nature or Krishna consciousness and make one's life perfect and successful. Being purified by one's intelligence and controlling the mind with determination; giving up the fruits of one's work; living in a secluded place; controlling one's body, mind and speech; being free from pride, lust and anger; and worshipping the Lord, one can be elevated to the position of self-realization. One who is transcendentally situated at once realizes the Supreme Brahman and becomes fully joyful. He is friendly towards every living entity.

When one understands Lord Krishna as the Supreme Person or Bhagavan by bhakti yoga, and when one is in Krishna consciousness, one enters into the kingdom of God. In all activities one should depend on Lord Krishna and work under His protection. If one becomes Krishna conscious, one overcomes all obstacles by His grace. The Supreme Lord is within everyone's heart as the Supersoul and He is directing the wanderings of all living entities, as if the living entities are on a machine. By surrendering unto the Supersoul, Lord Krishna, one can attain transcendental peace.

Lord Krishna gave this supreme instruction to Arjuna because Arjuna was His dear friend and devotee. He asked Arjuna to always think of Him, become His devotee, worship Him and offer homage to Him. He said that Arjuna should abandon all varieties of religion and just surrender to Him and become Krishna conscious. He promised to deliver him from all sins and fears. Lord Krishna said that this knowledge of Krishna consciousness should not be explained to non-devotees, but explaining this to devotees is as good as devotional service. Studying and listening to this sacred conversation of Krishna consciousness is also worshipping Krishna, and frees one from sinful reactions.

Lord Krishna asked Arjuna if his ignorance and illusions were dispelled after hearing the science of Krishna consciousness. Arjuna replied that he was now free from illusion and he had regained his memory (that he was a spirit soul and he should serve Krishna); he was firm and ready to fight.

Sanjaya overheard this divine conversation between Lord Krishna and Arjuna, and this message was so wonderful that his hair was standing on end. He took pleasure in being thrilled by every moment of it, and rejoiced again and again. Wherever there is Krishna, the Yogeshvara, and wherever there is Arjuna, there will certainly be opulence, victory, extraordinary power and morality.

Om tat sat.

Conclusion

If one wishes to be really happy, really successful, one must take to Krishna consciousness; there is no other alternative. If someone is not in Krishna consciousness, one will be in bodily consciousness, which is by nature false, unreal and full of anxiety. One will inevitably make mistakes after mistakes and success will be elusive. In His infinite mercy, Lord Sri Krishna Chaitanya Mahaprabhu gave mankind the sublime method of self-realization, namely chanting the Hare Krishna Maha Mantra so that we can be situated in our *svarupa* or constitutional position. Lord Krishna is our friend, our well-wisher. We are parts and particles of Him, like sparks of a big fire. Our only duty is to serve Him. We are born of God, so we must love Him. We can also help other living entities, such as cats, dogs, birds, fish, trees and insects by Krishna katha, and giving them *prasadam* and holy water (food and water offered to Krishna).

One must always strive to be in Krishna consciousness and perform all one's activities sincerely, purposefully and mindfully. This way one will live an anxiety-free, meaningful life in the material world, and one's transition to Goloka Vrindavana (Vaikuntha) life will be seamless. Because we are in material bodies, we should not neglect our worldly duties. We can convert material activities into spiritual activities by performing them for Krishna in Krishna consciousness (*yukta vairagya*). One must acquire health, wealth, knowledge and insight so that one can appositely use them in the service of the Lord. Because one's focus is on Krishna, one will easily acquire these qualities. There is no loss or diminution in executing Krishna consciousness. Even if one does not fully succeed in self-realization, one lives a pure life according to the four limbs of *dharma*: austerity, cleanliness, compassion and truth. Thus, one lives a life that is far superior to those of ordinary people. One will be a highly moral and worthy person, and continue on one's spiritual journey in the next life.

108 Questions and Answers

1. What is Krishna consciousness?

Krishna consciousness is the art of focusing one's attention on Krishna and giving one's love to Him. The awareness is of Krishna and nothing but Krishna. It is also absorbing one's awareness in thought of Krishna with deep affection. By chanting the Holy Names, one shifts one's consciousness from material consciousness to Krishna consciousness.

2. Who am I?

I am spirit soul, *aham Brahmasmi*, a part and parcel of the Supreme Lord.

3. Is there a God?

As I exist (Brahman) so there exists a Supreme Person (Parabrahman) whose name is Krishna. "*Krishnas tu Bhagavan svayam*"—SB 1.3.28.

4. Who is God?

God is Krishna, the most attractive and beautiful. Krishna means "most attractive." Krishna attracts us through His beauty as a flower attracts birds, bees and other pollinators.

5. Where do I go after death?

In general, we reincarnate into another body. If we are purified, we go to Goloka Vrindavana.

6. Why is Krishna blue?

The colour blue signifies infinity, like the sky and the ocean which are also blue.

7. Is God a person?

God is a person because we are persons and we come from God. God cannot be less than us in any aspect.

8. Will I be poor if I follow the path of bhakti?

Nobody becomes poor by following the path of bhakti yoga. Krishna has promised to carry what the devotee lacks and preserve what they have (BG 9.22).

9. What is the meaning or significance of life?

One must strive to be Krishna conscious and understand Krishna, oneself and one's relationship with Krishna.

10. What is the goal of life?

The goal of life is Krishna consciousness; to be situated in our original position as an eternal devotee of Krishna. We are part and parcel of Krishna. Our duty is to serve or worship Krishna, like the finger's duty is to serve the body, or a screw's purpose is to serve the entire machine.

11. Why are we here? Why are we born?

We are born to work out our karma and become Krishna conscious.

12. What is beyond the material world?

Beyond the material world is the spiritual world.

13. Why do we suffer and enjoy?

Our suffering is due to ignorance. Ignorance results from sinful activity (bad karma). Our enjoyment results from good karma or previous pious activities.

14. Why do the saints, *mahajans* and God allow suffering if they are powerful and able to remove it?

The material world is like a prison and the souls are here to work out karma before returning to Goloka Vrindavana. God and the *mahajans* do not want to change the character of the material world as it serves a purpose; however, individual souls are given benedictions to alleviate their suffering if they but choose to serve Krishna or God.

15. Will there always be misery?

There will always be misery in the material world because of the three *guna*s, but Krishna's devotees will be protected.

16. Why should we love Krishna?

Loving Krishna is natural, as a child loves his or her mother. Krishna is our Supreme Father and Mother.

17. Why should we please Krishna?

Pleasing Krishna gives pleasure to us, as feeding the stomach satisfies our whole body, or watering the roots of a plant (and not the leaves) supplies water to the whole plant.

18. Why should we worship Krishna?

Our duty and pleasure is to worship Krishna, as we are a fragmental part of the Supreme Whole, Krishna.

19. Why should we worship *only* Krishna?

Krishna says *"mam ekam saranam vraja"* (BG 18.66), which means worship only Me. He also tells us that those who worship the demigods will take birth among the demigods; those who worship Me, live with Me (BG 9.25). Even a demigod birth is not ideal because it is on the material plane and subject to the miseries of repeated birth and death. *The Srimad Bhagavatam* (3.32.2) also says not to worship demigods.

20. How do we transcend body consciousness?

Our soul is eternal and the body is impermanent. Reincarnation shows that the soul changes bodies as we change clothes. Understanding the impermanence of the body helps one transcend body consciousness.

21. What is the function of the spirit?

The function of the spirit is Krishna consciousness or bhakti.

22. Why is studying *The Bhagavad Gita* sufficient to become Krishna conscious?

The Bhagavad Gita is non-different from Krishna, and if one studies with devotion, sincerity and surrender, one becomes Krishna conscious, as did Arjuna.

23. Why should we study *The Bhagavad Gita*?

Studying *The Bhagavad Gita* removes ignorance directly, as in the case of Arjuna. By simply studying *The Bhagavad Gita* one can become Krishna conscious or self-realized.

24. What is *Brahma-jnana*?

Brahma-jnana is transcendental knowledge or Krishna consciousness.

25. What is the difficulty in being Krishna conscious?

There are no difficulties for a devotee after one has a higher taste, or *ruci*. Devotional service to Lord Krishna is very pleasurable. At the beginning of one's spiritual path, however, one needs to have discipline and put in effort with sincerity. "*Su-sukham kartum avyayam*": Krishna consciousness is pleasing (BG 9.2).

26. Why is the human form of life superior to a demigod's form of life?

We can work out our karma in the human form and be self-realized. A demigod's life is full of enjoyment, so the desire for Krishna consciousness (although possible) may not take place.

27. Why should we associate with Krishna and *mahajans*?

By keeping association with Krishna and *mahajans* through reading their words or reading about their lives and pastimes, we become Krishna conscious.

28. What does "yoga" mean?

"Yoga" means linking oneself with the Supreme or Krishna.

29. How do you link yourself with Krishna?

By chanting the Maha Mantra, meditation and breath control.

30. What is self-realization?

Self-realization means to know that I am a spirit soul, part and parcel of the Supreme Spirit (Supersoul or Krishna) and my duty is to serve Krishna as a part is meant to serve the whole.

31. What is the duty of a self-realized person?

He has no duty (*"tasya karyam na vidyate"*—BG 3.17), though he works to instruct others.

32. Who is an ideal person?

A devotee (Krishna conscious person) is ideal.

33. What is more powerful, the Holy Names or Krishna?

The Holy Names are more powerful because Krishna bestowed all powers in the Holy Names.

34. Is it good to do charitable work, such as opening hospitals and schools?

Not unless one is in Krishna consciousness. If performed in *sattva guna*, good karma is a result that is binding, leading to reincarnation. If performed for Krishna and His devotees, it will be transcendental and liberating.

35. Which is better, preaching in Krishna consciousness or doing mundane work in Krishna consciousness?

Both are equal as they are both done in Krishna consciousness.

36. Why does water taste good, and why is it refreshing?

Because Krishna is the taste of water (BG 7.8).

37. Why should one acquire knowledge?

By knowledge, such as of the Vedas, Krishna is to be known (BG 15.15). One should never stop learning.

38. How does one become the knower of everything?

By knowing Krishna one knows everything, because Krishna is omniscient (BG 15.19).

39. What is meant by "desirelessness"?

We should only have desires to serve Krishna.

40. Why should one be able to give precise answers to spiritual questions?

Sharp answers mean one has depth of knowledge, a higher level of consciousness and advancement.

41. How does ordinary consciousness change into Krishna consciousness?

Ordinary consciousness changes to Krishna consciousness with the realization that one is not the body, but spirit soul.

42. How does chanting bring about Krishna consciousness?

Chanting requires one to be in the present moment, in tune with Krishna.

43. What does "surrender" mean?

Obeying Krishna's instructions, as in *The Bhagavad Gita*, and being in tune with Krishna is surrender to Krishna. Realization that Krishna is the Controller, the Doer and the Owner of everything and everyone brings one to surrender.

44. How do we surrender to Krishna?

We surrender to Krishna by dovetailing our consciousness with the Supreme consciousness; one's activity becomes harmonious with Krishna's activities.

45. Why should we hear Krishna katha again and again?

Krishna katha keeps our knowledge of Krishna fresh and is also a purifying activity. Our soul hankers to hear about Krishna, and our soul becomes refreshed. *"Srnvatam sva-katha Krishna"*—SB 1.2.17.

46. Does one have to change or give up one's job to become Krishna consciousness?

No, one can perform one's occupational duty in Krishna consciousness and one can attain perfection. One does not have to go to a mountain or take *sannyas* (BG 18.46). One should remain where one is and dovetail all one's activities to Krishna. For example, one can rise early, take a shower, chant the Holy Names, and offer water, incense and flowers or lights to the deities before going to work. Throughout the day one can offer one's thoughts and activities to Krishna. All food can be offered to Krishna before eating, and one can go to the temple or listen to *kirtan,* and discuss Krishna katha with one's friends and family.

47. How does one become materially and spiritually successful?

One becomes materially and spiritually successful by pleasing Hari (*"samsiddhir hari tosanam"*—SB 1.2.13).

48. How does one purify oneself and become sinless?

One must understand one is not the body as the body is under the three modes of material nature. One does this by chanting the Holy Names, studying *shastra* and by eating *prasadam*. (BG 3.13, 4.21 and 7.28). We can dovetail our activities in Krishna consciousness.

49. How does one attain perfection?

By always thinking of Krishna, one becomes flawless and attains one's constitutional position.

50. What are the qualities one must have for spiritual progress?

One must be sincere, persevere and be enthusiastic.

51. Why does a Krishna conscious person become healthy, wealthy, wise and happy?

A devotee becomes Krishnized by devotional service. Thus he attains all Krishna's opulences.

52. Why are devotees vegetarian?

Devotees can eat only what Krishna eats, because they offer food to Krishna (*prasadam*). Food offered to Krishna is our real food. Krishna has instructed us on what he can accept to eat (B.G 9.26). Also, non-vegetarianism makes one cruel, and is not conducive to Krishna consciousness.

53. How do you know that God eats?

Because He said so: "*asnami*" (I eat), BG 9.26. "*Asan*," in Sanskrit, means "to eat," as related to "essen" (German), "enni" (Hungarian), "ăn" (Vietnamese), and many Indo-European languages. Sanskrit is the mother of languages.

54. What is the highest sacrifice?

Japa (BG 10.25).

55. What is the purpose of religion?

The purpose of religion is to understand and love Krishna.

56. What is the qualification to see God?

You must be a devotee of God to see Him.

57. What is omnipotent?

The name, form or anything related to Krishna is equally powerful as Krishna.

58. How does one find the meaning of life?

Connect with God through yoga and function in Krishna consciousness. Be a devotee and do whatever job you are doing (scientist, philosopher, worker, etc.).

59. How does one know one has found the meaning of life?

One has found the meaning of life when one progresses in Krishna consciousness and becomes content, joyful, healthy, wealthy and wise, and has a thrilling existence. One is a valuable person by oneself, like gold or gems.

60. What is the easiest way to become wealthy, famous, healthy or wise?

The easiest way is to become Krishna conscious, not by striving hard in the material world (BG 15.7).

61. How do we know the words of *The Bhagavad Gita* are true?

The words in *The Bhagavad Gita*, spoken by Krishna can't be false because Krishna or God is Absolute Truth, and His words, which emanate from Him, can therefore only be true. By the application of *The Bhagavad Gita*, or Krishna consciousness in our lives, we can experience that it is true.

62. How do we know that Krishna will take care of His devotees?

Because He says so in *The Bhagavad Gita*:

"Na me bhaktah pranasyati" (My devotee never perishes)—BG 9.31.

"yoga-kṣemaṁ vahāmy aham" (to them I carry what they lack, and I preserve what they have)—BG 9.22.

63. What is "buddhi yoga"?

When one progresses in Krishna consciousness, his intelligence becomes linked with Krishna and Krishna supplies transcendental intelligence to act correctly. Krishna will prompt from within (BG 10.10).

64. What is the astral body?

The astral body is made of the mind, intelligence and ego. When the physical body perishes, the astral body carries the soul to another body, which is called reincarnation.

65. What does "*Brahma bhuta*" mean?

Brahma bhuta means that one understands that one is spirit and exists eternally. This is the first step of self-realization and the same as Brahman realization.

66. Why is serving God essential?

Servience to God is our original quality, and we cannot be happy without service to God. If we don't water the roots of a tree, the other parts of the tree like the leaves and branches will die. If we don't supply food to the stomach, other parts of the body like the fingers or ears will die. (This is an example. We and God are eternal and never perish, but we will have no quality of life without God and will live a useless life, as good as dead.)

67. How does Krishna consciousness give solutions to all our problems?

Krishna is the Absolute Truth. When we are in touch with Krishna, all our problems are completely solved because we know the truth, and what to do.

68. How does one know God is our well-wisher?

Krishna is the friend of all living entities. *"Suhrdam sarva-bhutanam"* —BG 5.29.

69. Where does the term Krishna consciousness come from?

It comes from *The Bhagavad Gita*: *"man mana bhava,"* just be conscious of me—BG 9.34 and 18.65. This is Krishna consciousness.

70. What does "Bharata Varsa" mean?

"Bharata Varsa" means our whole planet earth (also Bharata Bhumi). The eldest son of Rsabha Deva was named Bharata, who was a great devotee with the best attributes. In his honour this planet became known as Bharata Varsa (SB 5.4.9). Today, the name "Bharat" is still used to refer to the sacred land of India, where Lord Krishna appeared.

71. What does *"Bharata bhumite haila manusya janma jara"* mean?

The quote is found in *The Chaitanya Charitamrita* (CC Adi. 9.41). These words were spoken by Sri Krishna Chaitanya Mahaprabhu, and mean that anyone born in a human body on this planet has a duty to become Krishna conscious. Bharata Bhumi means the earth planet, and the whole planet was known as Bharata Bhumi or India during Vedic times.

72. How does one keep Krishna in mind always?

By impressing the vision of the deities on one's heart and chanting the Holy Names.

73. Why should we offer food to Krishna every day?

Krishna is a person like us. Offer Him food, and He will eat. He gives us the opportunity to serve Him by feeding Him, and this purifies us and makes us happy.

74. Why should one begin Krishna consciousness at a young age, or as early as possible?

As one grows old, one accumulates karma and bad habits. One's consciousness gets polluted by living in the material world. Start the bhakti yoga process as soon as possible.

75. What is our biggest folly or sin?

Our biggest folly is that we disobey Krishna's instructions. One must obey God, *brahmanas*, devotees, the spiritual master and superiors such as the father and mother, otherwise there can be no success or perfection in life (BG 17.14).

76. What is the consequence of sin?

Total destruction, because one is no longer with Krishna (BG 3.32).

77. Should a self-realized person continue to do *tapa* (penance)?

Yes, *yajna* (sacrifice), *dana* (charity) and *tapa* (penance) should never be abandoned. They purify even the great souls (BG 18.5).

78. Why should one always be engaged in Krishna conscious activities?

Otherwise the mind may deviate and engage in mischief.

79. Why are spiritual people glowingly healthy and bright?

By spiritual practice one's body becomes healthy and glowing because by becoming spiritualized the body transcends the material. Old age and disease affect the material body, but not the spiritual body.

80. What makes people angry?

Thwarted desires make one angry (BG 3.37). This is the root of all anger.

81. How does one manifest positivity in their lives?

When one is in Krishna consciousness, all one's desires are automatically fulfilled. Be sincerely Krishna consciousness. Everything will come.

82. Why is a Krishna devotee's life always successful?

Krishna is always present in His devotee's heart. Krishna's presence gives one prosperity (*sri*), victory (*vijaya*), extraordinary power (*bhuti*), and morality or *niti* (BG 18.78). Krishna also says that for those who seek victory, He is morality (BG 10.38).

83. How does Krishna consciousness remove anxiety?

When the mind is absorbed in Krishna, no negative emotions can enter. When we chant the Holy Names, the Holy Names burn up the fog of anxiety. Realization that Krishna is the Controller and Doer removes the anxiety that our little self is in any trouble, for we have our best friend and well-wisher Krishna to protect and guide us.

84. How do we know we are Krishna conscious?

Our problems disappear and life becomes effortless. Anger, jealousy, and anxiety disappear. We see beauty around us. Everything converges in Krishna consciousness.

85. Can we change our fate?

Yes, we can change our fate by Krishna consciousness; otherwise our life is determined by our *guna* and karma.

86. How can we see God eye to eye?

The qualification for seeing God is Krishna consciousness.

87. Which is better, seeing Krishna or understanding Krishna?

Understanding Krishna is better, because knowing Krishna's nature, activities and words will transform us.

88. Why is human life a gift?

With a human body comes higher intelligence. One can become self-realized and know God (BG 18.70).

89. Who is a *mahatma*?

A *mahatma* is a pure devotee who is under the protection of Krishna (*"daivim prakrtim asritah"* — BG 9.13).

90. How does chanting, hearing and eating *prasadam* make one enlightened?

By chanting, hearing (or studying) and eating *prasadam,* we become directly in touch with Krishna. Touched by the Divine, we are immediately enlightened. One touches Krishna while performing all three activities. We are transformed, as a touchstone converts base metal into gold.

91. What is spiritual enlightenment?

By spiritual enlightenment one's true nature, the nature of the world, and one's relationship with Krishna and with other living entities all come into light. One clearly knows everything.

92. How does bringing Krishna into our heart make us enlightened?

If we can see the deities (Sri Sri Gaur Nitai, Sri Sri Radha Gopinath, Sri Jagannath, Baladeva and Subhadra, and Srila Prabhupada) in our heart, we become enlightened. Krishna is *sat-cit-ananda vigraha*. The deity and Krishna are non-different. The effulgence of the deity form fills our heart (Padma Purana).

93. What did Krishna teach Arjuna in *The Bhagavad Gita*?

Krishna taught *raja vidya*, the science of Krishna consciousness, to Arjuna. He specifically taught that we are not our bodies, but part and parcel of Krishna, and our duty is to be in tune with and serve Krishna.

94. Is it adequate to know who I am?

No, one must also act accordingly with the knowledge that one is not the body, but sprit soul.

95. What is the topmost knowledge?

Knowledge of Krishna, or Krishna consciousness is the most royal knowledge (*raja vidya, raja gujya*).

96. What is the most sublime and pure knowledge?

It is the knowledge of Krishna consciousness: that we are not the body, but part and parcel of Krishna; we have to dovetail our consciousness with the Supreme consciousness; our duty is to serve Him. We must perform all our activities in Krishna consciousness.

97. What is our real duty?

Our duty is to serve Krishna.

98. How does a devotee become a knower of everything?

By knowing Krishna, one comes to know everything (BG 15.19). Knowledge of Krishna consciousness reveals everything, like the sun lights up the sky (BG 5.16).

99. What is our normal condition?

Our most normal condition is Krishna consciousness. If one is not in Krishna consciousness, one is not sane. In Krishna consciousness we are in our eternal self; we are full of knowledge and bliss. Also, we are then healthy, wealthy, wise and happy.

100. What is transcendental activity?

Any work sanctioned by Krishna and done in Krishna consciousness (BG 3.31).

101. How can our life be made perfect?

Our life can be perfect by being in Krishna consciousness. The more we align ourselves with our essence, the better we live our lives. We become happy (content and self-aware), energetic, lively and see beauty in nature and in all living entities. We rediscover our eternal, knowledgeable and blissful existence.

102. How can one live a happy worldly life?

By being Krishna conscious one lives happily on earth physically, but spiritually in Goloka Vrindavana. Later, when the spirit leaves the body, then one lives eternally in Goloka Vrindavana.

103. How long does it take to become Krishna conscious?

One can become Krishna conscious in a moment, or over many years, or births (BG 7.19). The transition from body consciousness to Krishna conscious depends on one's sincerity and *sadhana*.

104. What is pure ego and false ego?

Pure ego is the self, *aham Brahmasmi*. False ego is thinking one is the body.

105. What is a prescribed duty?

Prescribed duty means occupational duty, such as a farmer's duty is to farm. We must perform these duties as a form of *tapa*, which builds character.

106. What does "*achintya-bheda-abheda*" mean?

"*achintya-bheda-abheda*" is Lord Sri Krishna Chaitanya Mahaprabhu's philosophy that we are simultaneously the same and different from God or Krishna. After self-realization, one eternally remains a devotee of Krishna.

107. How did Krishna console the *gopis* (milkmaids)?

Krishna consoled the *gopis* by telling them that whenever they think of Him, they are never separated from Him.

108. Where does the number 108 come from?

The number 108 is very auspicious. The number of *gopis* in Vrindavana is 108, and that is why we chant the Maha Mantra on a string of 108 beads. The principle bead signifies Lord Krishna. There are 108 Upanishads. In the body, there are 108 energy centers or chakras. Astronomically, the distance between the sun and the earth is 108 times the diameter of the sun.

Glossary

Abhyas: practice

Acarya: teacher who teaches by example

Adhyatmic: relating to the soul

Ahimsa: nonviolence

Aisvarya: wealth

Ananda: joy or bliss

Aparadha: offenses

Aparigraha: not accepting gifts

Arati: offering lights to Krishna

Artha: distressed

Artharthi: desirer of wealth

Asana: a steady comfortable posture

Asteya: not stealing

Atma: soul

Atmarama: self-satisfied

Bhaga: opulence

Bhagavan: God with six opulences

Bhakti: devotion

Bhakti's nine processes:

1. *Sravanam*: hearing
2. *Kirtanam*: devotional chanting
3. *Vishnu smaranam*: remembering
4. *Pada sevanam*: serving the Lotus feet of the Lord
5. *Archanam*: worshipping
6. *Vandanam*: praying

7. *Dasyam*: serving
8. *Sakhyam*: friendship
9. *Atma nivedanam*: surrendering

Bhava: divine emotion

Brahma: creator God

Brahma bhuta: self realized

Brahmacharya: celibacy

Brahman: impersonal aspect of God

Brahmana pathi: path of self realization

Brahmanda: cosmic egg (the universe)

Brahma nirvana: liberation in Brahman

Bodhi citta: enlightened mind

Buddhi: divine intelligence, intelligence linked to Krishna

Chakra: wheel or power center in the spine

Cit: knowledge or consciousness

Chintamani: the crest jewel of thought

Dama: self-control

Dana: charity

Daya: compassion

Dehi: who lives in the body (soul)

Deity: the form of the Lord made of stone, metal or wood

Desha: space, land

Dhama: abode

Dharma: duty, order of God, cosmic law, essential quality, for example, heat is the *dharma* of fire

Dhira: steady
Dhyana: meditation
Dhyani: meditator
Divyacaksu: divine eyes
Guna: three modes (*sattva*, *raja*, *tama*)
Hari: the stealer of hearts (Krishna)
Janma: birth
Japa: chanting the Holy Names on a mala of 108 beads
Jara: old age
Jijnasa: inquisitive
Jiva: living entity
Jnana: knowledge of God
Jnani: wise
Jivan-mukta: liberated while living
Jyoti: light
Kala: time
Kalpa-taru: wish-fulfilling tree
Karma: sum total of one's work
Karmi: materialistic worker
Kirtan: singing or chanting the Lord's Name
Kripa: mercy or kindness
Kshetra: field
Lobha: greed
Loka: planets
Laulya: divine greed

Mahajan: pure devotee, a great soul (also called a *mahatma*)

Maha Mantra: the great Hare Krishna mantra: *Hare Krishna, Hare Krishna, Krishna Krishna, Hare Hare, Hare Rama, Hare Rama, Rama Rama, Hare Hare*

Maya: divine illusion, Durga Devi

Mogha: futile

Moksha: liberation

Mrityu: death

Mudha: foolish

Nistha: fixed

Niyama: rules

Om: the transcendental sound representation of Brahman, Brahma-jyoti, and Shabda-Brahman or the Holy Names

Om tat sat: om is Truth

Paramatma: Supersoul

Para vritti: awakening

Prajna: insight, intuition

Pranayama: breath control

Prasadam: food offered to Krishna (purified)

Pratyahara: withdrawing the senses inward

Prema: love for Krishna

Raja: passion

Ruci: taste

Sadhaka: spiritual aspirant

Sadhana: spiritual practice

Samadhi: transcending the material ego, opening the Sahasrara chakra or Krishna consciousness

Samsara: material world

Sankalpa: resolute determination

Santosha: contentment in all circumstances

Sarthak: successful

Sat: truth (also *Satyam*)

Sattva: goodness

Saucha: cleanliness

Shakti: power

Shastra: scripture

Shiva: the destructive god, auspiciousness

Shraddha: strong faith or inclination

Siddha: perfected being

Sila: good conduct

Smriti: memory

Sriya: beauty

Svadhyaya: study by one's effort and introspection

Svarupa: constitutional position or form

Tama: ignorance

Tapa: austerity

Vairagya: detachment

Vani: spoken message

Vapu: physical body

Vibhuti: opulence

Vidya: knowledge

Vigraha: form
Vijnana: science
Viryasya: strength
Vishnu: maintainer God
Vyadhi: disease
Yajna: sacrifice in relation to God
Yama: restraint
Yasha: fame
Yoga: connection with the Supreme
Yuga: age (era); Satya, Treta, Dvapara, Kali

My Story

I am over 65 years old and in a male Bengali body, but I know that I am a universal person and do not associate with my place of birth. My life is successful. I am happy. My mind is, for the most part centered on Krishna. I do not experience anxiety; I am happy and content. My mind is quiet and I can see clearly. I am so grateful to be where I am. It has been a long journey when I think of where I started and where I am now. A devotee should always be ready for the disappearance of the material body because the soul continues eternally. Krishna should be foremost in one's mind (by chanting, studying or worshipping), and daily duties should also be done as an offering to Krishna. A devotee's body, mind, and soul belong to Krishna because when one becomes a devotee, one voluntarily surrenders to Krishna. Do not wish for death or life, and rather serve Krishna and be happy.

I keep myself in *sattva guna* by keeping clean in body and mind, bathing, eating *prasadam*, reading *The Bhagavad Gita*, and cultivating good habits. I have a daily routine, which includes awakening at approximately 5 a.m. I chant before a small breakfast, take a shower, listen to some Prabhupada lectures and a chapter of *The Bhagavad Gita*. Around noon, I cook some *prasadam*. In the afternoon, I do some household work, study about spiritual or chemistry topics, or read about current events. In the evening, I often watch Mayapur TV and retire for the night.

When I came across the poem *Boro Kripa Koile Krishna* by Srila Prabhupada for the first time, tears came to my eyes. I felt the truth, that Krishna has bestowed His mercy on me. How could I be where I am without Lord Krishna's mercy? How would I be healthy, wealthy, wise and happy?

We can monitor our progress on the spiritual path by Sri Rupa Goswami's ontology. First there is inclination, faith (*shraddha*). From early childhood, I had an interest in spirituality. I grew up in rural Bengal, where I felt a close connection to nature. I was surrounded by fields and water. When I was about six years old, once on a sunny beautiful day, I saw a most wonderful dragonfly. I observed the reflecting colours of the dragonfly and was amazed by the beauty of the insect, the day, the sky, and I felt a loving pang in my heart. Spontaneously I thought of Bhagavan. I wished to see God. During the evenings a neighbour would come to our house to read from the Ramayana. The stories were egrossing and I listened with rapt attention, getting transported to the spiritual realms. On Thursdays I used to perform Laxmi puja assisted by my younger sister, Bithi.

I have always enjoyed reading about saints. We can associate with devotees physically and mentally by reading about the lives and written words of saints. We study *vanis* of *sadhus* of earlier times through books about and by saints. Throughout my life I have researched and found a path, which changed over time, that I believed would help me to find God.

When I was in grade four, I came across a book called *Bharater Sadhaka* (The Saints of India). Therein I read the story of Buddha and I was deeply impressed. I was amazed by the analogy given to describe Lord Buddha. The earth was once covered by clouds and every living being was living in darkness. There were some high mountains, however, that had their peaks above the clouds. Buddha, unlike others, lived in the light, as the peaks of the high mountains pierced through the clouds. Buddha taught that one should practice *dharma*, speak the truth, meditate and not harm any living entity.

When I grew up even more, in my adolescent years, I learnt about Swami Vivekananda and how he influenced the West with the wisdom of Indian spirituality. He also taught that one can be in higher consciousness of mind by meditation, and that by *brahmacharya* one can have a great memory.

Later, I read about Ramakrishna, the guru of Swami Vivekananda from *The Gospel of Sri Ramakrishna*. It was written by M. Sri Ramakrishna, who taught about spirituality in a very simple manner, with practical examples. Later still, I came across *Autobiography of a Yogi* by Paramahansa Yogananda and followed kriya yoga meditation, but was not fully satisfied with the impersonal concept of God. How can one have a loving relationship with light?

One day I happened to come to the Hare Krishna temple with my family. I was deeply attracted to the deities in the temple, and was amazed by the beautiful Bengali song *Kabe Habe Balo Se Din Amar*, being sung by a devotee in the temple. Later, we visited the temple many times and my entire family had happy experiences in the temple with *arati*, spiritual discourse and *prasadam*. Enjoying deity worship and Krishna katha (*sadhu sanga*) is another step in the progress of one's *sadhana*. I started to chant 16 rounds (to be increased later) of the Holy Names on a daily basis: *Hare Krishna, Hare Krishna, Krishna Krishna, Hare Hare, Hare Rama, Hare Rama, Rama Rama, Hare Hare.*

I then started to have spiritual dreams of devotees singing and chanting the Maha Mantra. I dreamt of Srila Prabhupada, Paramahansa Yogananda and Krishna under a tamal tree in blue light. I had the dream of Krishna under a tamal tree after reading a poem, *Agre Dirgha Taro 'yam Arjuna*. In the poem a traveler asks for direction, and is directed to the village of cowherd boys, where under the tamal tree groves, a bluish cowherd boy plays His flute on the bank of the river Yamuna; He will show the path. Seeing Krishna in a dream is as good as seeing Krishna in a wakeful state. I had many insights into Krishna consciousness which lead to a deeper understanding of Krishna, which is also as good as seeing Krishna. Krishna is present in His name and the deity form, so when chanting the Holy Names or looking at deities, one is in direct contact with Krishna.

I made a pilgrimage to Mayapur and Vrindavana with my family, and returned with some reading material provided at Vrindavana in the MVT residence. I read *Krishna: A Reservoir of Pleasure*, and then found and listened to the audiobook on YouTube. While on YouTube, I found other books that were read aloud, and listened to *Raja Vidya*. After hearing these books, I felt I had understood the essence of Krishna consciousness, and was in a very happy state for a few weeks. My consciousness transitioned from body to soul consciousness. I understood that all things material or spiritual, including us, emanate from Lord Krishna. We are not bodies, but spirit souls. On earth, we have a material experience, but we are spiritual beings and our lives' duty is to be dovetailed in the service of Lord Krishna.

Our life is meaningless without Krishna consciousness.

www.ingramcontent.com/pod-product-compliance
Lightning Source LLC
Chambersburg PA
CBHW050906160426
43194CB00011B/2310